Cinema Beyond the Danube:
The Camera and Politics

by

MICHAEL JON STOIL

The Scarecrow Press, Inc.
Metuchen, N.J.   1974

Library of Congress Cataloging in Publication Data

Stoil, Michael Jon, 1950-
    Cinema beyond the Danube: the camera and politics.

    Bibliography: p.
    1. Moving-pictures--Europe, Eastern--History.
2. Moving-pictures--Political aspects. I. Title.
PN1993.5.E82S8   791.43'0947   74-5274
ISBN 0-8108-0722-X

To

My father and mother

TABLE OF CONTENTS

v

TABLE OF ILLUSTRATIONS

INTRODUCTION

The writings of Soviet bloc specialists on cinema in Eastern Europe sometimes read as if these social scientists have never seen an Eastern European film. Too often, they discuss the use of motion pictures as propaganda without going into sufficient detail on individual films or even on major trends in the style and content of motion picture propaganda. Occasionally, they commit gross errors; one "scholar" insisted that the major Soviet director of the 1920's was Einstein rather than Eisenstein. In general, these authorities are satisfied with generalizations on the use of films in the "political socialization process"--a euphemism for political education--while totally neglecting the actual state of the art.

Film critics who have specialized in Eastern European film history often go to the opposite extreme. They tend to neglect the special social and political context in which the film-makers of the area must work. Too often, they analyze the artistic aspects of film at the expense of its social significance. This is an error in judgment. Eastern Europe is not the West; the politics of the region, the administration of the film industry and the contents of the Eastern European motion picture are closely interwoven. Almost all Eastern European films, including the most inane musicals, fulfill a political purpose. A neglect of this aspect of the cinema of the region is a neglect of more than half the meaning and significance of the films. Nevertheless, film critics have tended to commit this sin of omission in book after book and review after review. It is clear that the critics and the Soviet area specialists are not talking to each other.

In this volume I am combining film criticism with political and social analyses to provide a more complete picture of Eastern European cinema. This book is written primarily for those with little or no knowledge of the history of film-making in Eastern Europe so that it can be used successfully as an introductory text on the subject. It differs from other textbooks because of its emphasis on the social significance of film. For this reason, I consider it to be of value to both social science students and to those students of film who have previously lacked the necessary area study background to fully appreciate Eastern European works.

For the purpose of this study, the film history of the Soviet Union and the other Communist states of Eastern Europe will be considered separately. These "other" states are Poland, Czechoslovakia, Hungary, Yugoslavia, Bulgaria, Romania and Albania. I will not discuss the cinema of the German Democratic Republic, although it is politically within the orbit of the Soviet Union, because the cultural traditions of East Germany, especially in motion pictures, are Western rather than East European.

ACKNOWLEDGMENTS

I wish to thank Pam Wintle of the American Film Institute of Washington, D. C., Williard Van Dyke and Charles Silver of the Museum of Modern Art of New York City for making their collections and libraries available to me. I also wish to thank my grandmother, Mrs. Dora Stoil, for her help in translating vital material from the original Russian.

Finally, I wish to acknowledge the advice and encouragement given to me by Dr. Andrew Gyorgy and Miss Alicija Szydlowska, both of the Institute of Sino-Soviet Studies of the George Washington University. In some ways, this is their book as well as mine.

CHAPTER 1

THE SOCIALIST FILM INDUSTRY

It is common practice, in the Soviet Union, to encourage the development of uniquely "socialist" methods for
historical analysis, scientific investigation and other creative
fields. This practice goes to the extent that certain psychi-
atric treatments are out of official favor in the Soviet Union
because they supposedly contradict the basis for Marxist
theory. For the Communist Party ideologists, the practice
is worthwhile because it demonstrates the applicability of
Marxist theory and analysis to all areas of knowledge. In
addition, it underscores the differences between the "reactionary" West and the "progressive" Soviet Union. A
similar situation is reported to exist in China, with the sub-
stitution of Maoist thought for the Soviet brand of ideology.

Communist societies, however, cannot develop their
own, uniquely "socialist" methods for film-making. For
example, the use of modern tricolor processing for making
color films was delayed in the "progressive" Soviet Union
until German technicians skilled in the use of Agfacolor
could be rescued from Nazi studios. The difficulty in developing a "socialist" color process or any "socialist" film-
making technique is that film production is a highly complex
union of several technical arts. Because of this, American
film-makers trying to make a profit and Soviet film-makers
trying to make a point must use identical methods to solve
the identical problems. The only divergences from "Western"
film-making that technology will permit are in the censorship
of scenarios and the administration of the studio. In these
two areas, however, the Soviet methods are not as unique
as they might have been. Soviet film studio organization,
for example, was revised in 1936 to consciously imitate the
more efficient organization of Hollywood studios.

The Technical Elements of Soviet Film

The essential elements of the art of modern film-

1

making are cinematography--the use of the motion picture
camera--editing, sound technology, color process, scenario
writing and acting. In addition to these six are a host of
supporting crafts such as set design, costuming, musical
direction and special effects, all of which are used as soon
as the subject of the film strays from stark realism. To
unite these diverse elements into a coherent work has traditionally been the task of the film director. The film director, or "regisseur," as he is known in Europe and the
Soviet Union, is supervised and supplied by the administrative organization of the producer, who is known in the
socialist states as the "studio director."

The six elements of film-making are virtually universal in every film-producing country, although the level
of technology available varies from country to country.
Color photography, for example, can be found today in all
of its levels of development, from the simple tricolor process first applied thirty years ago and still used in India,
to the most advanced versions of Technicolor seen in 2001:
A Space Odyssey.

The most essential of the six basic elements of film-
making is cinematography. The history of cinematography
is the development of creative applications of changing camera technology. In its earliest use, around 1900, the primitive motion picture camera was firmly fixed in front of a
stage set in order to record a performance from a fixed
position. The effect was similar to being a spectator at a
play, seeing the action from only one perspective. This
technique was successful in holding the audience's attention
only while cinema remained a novelty because, as art, it
was insipid and boring.

The introduction of the mobile film camera changed
this; it permitted the action to be viewed from more than
one angle. By 1905, it was discovered that different lenses
and camera speeds could produce a large selection of perspective. With such innovations as the geography shot,
slow motion, time-lapse sequences and, above all, the close-
up, the audience's attention could be directed to a particular
segment of the total action or vast crowd scenes could be
shown from many points of view, making a few hundred
actors look like tens of thousands to the amazed spectators.
In 1908, the Turin Studios of Italy produced The Last Days
of Pompeii, using all of the "latest" camera techniques.
This early spectacle, with its primitive special effects

volcano and its surging mobs of doomed "Romans," made
film-makers aware of the possibilities of film to recreate
history.   Seven years later, D. W. Griffith's Birth of a
Nation demonstrated that history could be rewritten for propaganda purposes and still be presented so realistically that
the audience became emotionally involved with the characters
in the film.   It was a very popular film in the Soviet Union.

The Soviet Union has not contributed greatly to the
development of camera technique or special camera effects.
However, Soviet film-makers during the 1920's were the great
innovators in the second essential element of film--editing.
Film editing is the process of joining together separate pieces
of film to create a coherent work.   Editing is used to im-
prove the pace of films, to move from one scene to another,
to imply changes of time and space, and to provide a montage of images that, when viewed as a whole, create a desired intellectual or emotional effect.   To the creative director, such as Jean-Luc Godard, "editing is the supreme
touch of direction. "

The original theories behind the use of editing as
part of the creative process were all formulated in the
Soviet Union during the early 1920's.   In his book, On Film
Technique, Vsevolod Pudovkin expounded the theory that
editing should be the combining of individual sequences of
film to create an impression of the film's action or a character's personality.   In his well known example, a brief
shot of a sleeping kitten is immediately followed by a shot
of a tramp preparing to throw a stone and then a third shot
of the tramp and the kitten together, showing their proximity.
This sequence clearly demonstrates the tramp's malicious
personality.   A much more dynamic theory of editing was
devised by Pudovkin's friendly artistic rival, Sergei Eisenstein.   Eisenstein maintained that the editing montage effect
was based on a collision of clashing images to create an
emotional effect.

Russian editing theories have been studied and copied
throughout the world, much as Russian technicians have
studied and copied other technical aspects of film-making
that first appeared in the late 1920's and the 1930's.   Neither
sound nor color processes for the cinema were invented independently in the Soviet Union, despite recent Russian
claims.   Sound was introduced in the Soviet studio in 1930,
during the First Five Year Plan.   Despite the slogan, "Produce Everything from Soviet Materials!" the first sound

equipment had to be imported from Germany. After the
equipment was installed, lack of training and expertise in its
use resulted in disaster after disaster, including the destruction of some of the expensive apparatus, until German technicians arrived to train the Soviet technical staff. The transformation of the German Agfacolor color process into the
Russian Sovcolor process after World War II has a similar
history of early failures.

In the less technical arts associated with film-making,
the Soviet Union and Eastern Europe have usually been as
accomplished as the studios in the West. Because of early
experience with costume dramas and a taste for the exotic,
Soviet costuming has maintained a high level of authenticity
and imagination. Music in Soviet sound films, on the average, has been superior to the Hollywood product, primarily
due to the policy of incorporating the talents of the best composers, such as Dmitri Shostakovitch and Sergei Prokofiev,
into the popular feature films. A secondary explanation of
the Soviet studio's expertise in film music is the early development of motion picture musicals in the Soviet Union.

Early Soviet experiments in set design had almost as
great an impact on world cinema as the Russian film editing
theories. The concept of "constructivism"--the use of simple, black-and-white sets to imply locations rather than depict them--was a topic of heated discussions at the film institutes' commissary tables when Eisenstein and Pudovkin
were still students. The science fiction film Aelita (1924)
has been praised as an example of pure expressionist set
design. This experimentation in design ended, however,
with the imposition of strict party control over the studios
at the end of the decade. The theories of set design and,
to a lesser extent, of editing, were condemned as "intellec-
tualism" and the early innovators were forced to revert to
conventional methods in these arts.

The art of animation is often treated as the stepchild
of the cinema. Animation can best be defined as the use of
graphics in motion pictures and has been an important art
form in the Soviet Union and Eastern Europe since 1936, the
year in which the animation division of the Moscow State
Film Institute was established. Although animation in the
Soviet Union has been used almost exclusively for children's
entertainment, animated films are frequently geared to adult
audiences in the other countries of Eastern Europe. Polish
animators have been active in adult satires and surrealist

works, possibly because the regime has tended to be less
critical of surrealism in cartoons than in other art forms.
In Prague, directors have pioneered in the use of animation
as special effects in feature films. An excellent example
of this was The Fabulous World of Jules Verne (1958), in
which the live actors appeared to be sailing through the sea
and air in machines taken directly from the illustrations in
Jules Verne's early editions. Yugoslavia has been the most
prolific and most innovative of the nations of Europe in the
production of animated films for the adult audience. The
Zagreb school of animation has given us the work of Vlado
Kristl, Vatroslav Mimica and the satires of Dusan Vukotic,
the first foreign animation director to win an Oscar.

Today, Soviet and Eastern European technicians are
among the most skilled and talented working in cinema. War
and Peace (1967), for example, is a masterpiece of technical
arts in everything except its English dubbing. Nevertheless,
Soviet technical methods have not been innovative, except in
costuming, editing and design. Neither of the two last-men-
tioned arts has advanced in the Soviet Union to the extent that
the West has advanced in cinematography and other allied
crafts. The major recent innovations in film-making in the
socialist countries have been in animation, and none of this
originality stems from the Soviet Union.

Scenario Writing in the Soviet Union

Writing for films has less to do with technology than
the other elements of film-making. Despite this, early cinema had little or nothing to do with the written word. It
was common practice in the days of silent film for a director
to decide upon a plot and then film it, ad libbing the details
while the camera was turning. In this way, motion pictures
that grossed thousands of dollars, marks or rubles could be
completed in very little time.

Alexander Korda, the great British producer, explained
that his first film as a director in Hungary was based on a
story he made up sitting in a cafe on the day before shooting.
For the next three days, he dragged his star and his camera-
man around wartime Budapest, filming mock battles staged
on the Hungarian Army's drillground for his benefit. The
movie, a simple melodrama with a military setting, grossed
several hundred times the cost of production--which was min-
imal--and made an instant star out of Korda's leading player.

Not once during the frantic four days of production did Korda or anyone else write anything approximating a plot.

D. W. Griffith modified this pattern by creating the modern feature film. When producers were spending hundreds of thousands of dollars to make films of an hour or longer in length, it was impossible to direct a scene without at least some idea of what action would follow it. Plots quickly became complex, involving complicated literary devices such as foreshadowing and symbolism. This did not give as large an opportunity to the scenario writers as could have been expected. Throughout the remainder of the silent era, directors continued to write their own scenarios, sometimes with the help of writing assistants. Often, as in the case of Pudovkin's silent work, films were completed without a true script; the directors and actors worked from a detailed plot outline with notes scribbled on it to instruct the cameramen.

The practice of making a feature film without a script provided problems for potential censors. A censorship board might reject the subject of a film as being too controversial or, in the case of the Soviet Union, as being too bourgeois. In general, however, a censorship board has to wait until filming and editing is completed before passing judgment on the director's work unless they have a scenario to spell out the exact content of the film. During the early 1920's, Soviet censors were reluctant to completely discard films that were defective in their ideological content. Although the Party officials could demand that ideologically offensive scenes could be edited out and more suitable sequences added, their inability to reuse the expensive film and their limited ability to determine the propaganda content of a film before it was completed gave a comparatively large amount of intellectual freedom to the directors. Clearly, if the ruling Communist Party wished to exercise a complete control over the content of Soviet films, its monopoly of the distribution of films was inefficient and wasteful.

The control over the propaganda content of films was partially achieved by having reliable party members observe the filming, but this practice was often ineffective. The content of films is too easily changed in the cutting room by a skillful film editor. Complete control could not be achieved until the introduction of sound.

Sound required a written script before filming was

begun, for several reasons. Sound meant dialogue and dialogue meant that actors had to memorize their lines and cues
before they set foot on the sound stage. The use of sound
equipment also prevented the director from shouting directions to the actors and the crew in the middle of filming.
All of the film studio personnel had to know exactly what to
do at any given moment, and only a detailed scenario could
supply this degree of coordination. Finally, the use of sound
very quickly led to the use of music. The music director
and the composer had to know the exact sequence of action
and the length of time for scenes in order to score the film.

As sound began to force the use of detailed scenarios
written before filming, ideological control and censorship became practical on a widespread basis. Lowered costs for
Soviet-made film and equipment also aided the censors by allowing them to forget the economic loss of banning already
completed motion pictures. Finally, the various party controls were supplemented by purging politically unreliable film
workers from the motion picture industry and replacing them
with good Party men. From the early 1930's until the present, the only way that a Soviet director could remain a director has been to walk carefully the unsteady tightrope of
ideological "correctness," sacrificing artistic principles to
the changing trends in official propaganda.

The modern practice of submitting a script to a feature film studio is primarily a process of herding the script
through several censorship barriers. First, of course, the
author of the script must be a member of the Writer's Union
in good standing, a guarantee that the author is not totally
out of favor with the regime. Secondly, the writer submits
the script to the studio director who is the administrative
head of a motion picture studio in the socialist countries,
not to be confused with the regisseur or film director. The
studio director, however, has only limited authority and must
submit the script to the head of the studio's Party apparatus.
If the local Party leader approves, or approves with revi-.
sions, a budget is prepared and submitted with the scenario
to the State Committee for Cinematography. When the State
Committee approves, production can begin. Thus, government consorship over a film is well established even before
the production is casted.

As soon as a segment of the film is completed, the
scene is shown to the administrators, who are encouraged
to make criticisms of the film's ideological shortcomings.

These shortcomings must be repaired, of course, and this requires alterations in the scenario and several retakes. When the completed segments are filmed and spliced together, there are additional preview showings, first before the studio administration and ultimately before a high level Party delegation. Again, the "critics" may demand revisions or even the cancelling of the film completely. This was precisely what happened to Sergei Eisenstein's Bezhin Meadow, a very expensive sound spectacular that was unfortunately completed immediately after the Party had changed its ideological viewpoint on the film's subject. If the completed film is approved by the Party delegates, it can be released, subject to condemnation in the future if changes in the regime's official ideology should make the work obsolete.

These conditions, although partly true for every socialist state, have been carried to extreme lengths only in the Soviet Union and, probably, in Bulgaria and Albania. In the other socialist societies of Eastern Europe, Party supervision of scenarios tends to be less bureaucratic. Czechoslovakia and Poland, for example, have returned to the practice of allowing directors to write their own scenarios, saving considerable time and money while permitting greater artistic unity. Yugoslavia's censorship of films is designed primarily to prevent overt criticism of the regime and protect the citizens from what the regime considers pornography. There is no state supervision to ensure sufficient propaganda content, as there is in the Soviet Union.

Managing a Socialist Film Industry

The film industry, like almost every other enterprise in a socialist society, is considered to be an integral part of the economy. The most successful control of film in the Soviet Union has been accomplished through economic administration of the studio. Naturally, the amount of economic control varies throughout Eastern Europe depending on the degree of "pure" socialism achieved, but the threat of a sudden tug on the budget pursestrings is present in the mind of every film-maker of the area.

In countries where Five-Year plans exist, the annual budgets for film studios must be approved years in advance. This creates the unique situation of studios receiving money for the production of films that have not yet been slated for production. Allotments of men and material to the

photochemical and optical equipment industries are supposed
to be planned in coordination with the projected number and
budgets of future film production. Clearly, if the planning
system worked, it would have to be a masterpiece of efficiency and coordination.

The problem is that the attempt to synchronize feature
film production to the Five-Year Economic Plans does not
work except, perhaps, in a state like Bulgaria where feature
film production is still very limited. The need to rewrite
and retake scene after scene for ideological reasons makes
budget overruns the rule rather than the exception. In Poland
and Czechoslovakia today, as in the Soviet Union twenty years
ago, the relative scarcity of production facilities and available
production equipment--sound booms, copying machines and
even 16mm cameras--forces rival production teams to share
the facilities and equipment. This can create conflicts: one
production company kept from using its sound equipment because another company is hammering props to the stage in
the next room, another company bickering over the use of
extras for a crowd scene with a fourth company which has
"borrowed" them for the day. This kind of activity leads to
additional delays. Even when film-makers are able to keep
to their production schedule and budget, it is rarely possible
to insure that the chemical and equipment supply industries
can keep to theirs.

Under Stalin, the failure of the motion picture industry to maintain the budgets and schedules of the Five-Year
Plans was attributed to "sabotage" and sloppy administration.
Studio directors were removed frequently for inefficiency,
sometimes tainted with permitting "savage veteran spies,
Trotskyite and Bukharinist agents ... to wreck the Soviet
movie industry. " The relationship of the industry to the
government was changed an average of once every six years.
A Ministry of the Cinema existed from 1947 until 1953 when
it was absorbed by the newly created Ministry of Culture.
Nine years later, a Central Administration for the Production
of Films received the control of all aspects of the motion
picture industry, although remaining nominally under the
Ministry of Culture. Most of the other socialist states followed suit. In Czechoslovakia, Rumania, Poland and Hungary, the administration of the motion picture industry remains an autonomous preserve under the national ministries
of culture. In the Soviet Union, however, the motion picture
industry was given increased governmental status in 1965
when a State Committee for Cinematography was created

under the direct supervision of the ruling Council of Ministers. This raised the status of the film industry to a quasi-ministry level.

In 1973, the tsar of Soviet cinema was Aleksei V. Romanov, who became the first Chairman of the State Committee for Cinematography in 1963 at the age of fifty-seven. Romanov's career before receiving this position had nothing to do with films or film-making. Until the 1960's, he was a journalist, usually associated with the editorial staffs of the Leningrad press. In 1961, he became a candidate member of the Central Committee of the Communist Party and Deputy Chief of the committee's Ideological Department. His appointment as head of the film industry reveals the importance which the Party still attaches to the propaganda content of Soviet films.

The Socialist Film Institutes

Perhaps the one unquestioned benefit of state control of the motion picture industry has been the establishment of systematic educational programs in almost all of the Communist states of Eastern Europe. The oldest of these is the Moscow State Film Institute, founded in 1919. The Institute was open initially to any young Russian who had demonstrated theatrical ability and was able to convince a member of the teaching staff that he had potential in some aspect of film-making. The Institute was organized into classes open to all of its students and film-making workshops centered on the handful of pre-war film directors who had opted to remain in Russia after the Revolution. Some of these workshops remained intact after their students had graduated; the troupe of Sergei Yutkevitch managed to escape the purges and continued to produce films well into the 1940's.

By 1930, however, the Moscow State Film Institute had fallen under stricter ideological control. Although it remained open to non-Party members, participation in Komsomol--the Party-sponsored youth movement--became a near prerequisite for admission. Courses in film-making technology and acting techniques are now heavily supplemented with ideological training. As if the official courses in Marxism-Leninism were insufficient, the young Party members at the Institute insure that the students spend vacations at "voluntary" seminars in various aspects of communism. The Moscow State Film Institute, with its smaller associate

institutes in Leningrad and Kiev, have evolved from the artists' workshop concept into training academies for future
Soviet propagandists. Nevertheless, the three Soviet institutes continue to provide an excellent education in film techniques from experienced directors and actors. For this reason, the State Film Institutes are often admired by would-be
film-makers struggling to obtain experience and recognition
in the West.

After the Second World War, institutes of film-making
patterned after the Moscow State Film Institute were created
at Budapest in Hungary, Lodz in Poland, and Prague in
Czechoslovakia. Of these, Lodz was the first to establish
a reputation as a technical school equal to that of the Moscow institute. By 1957, Lodz had surpassed its prototype
in the important task of instilling a creative spirit in its
students. Among the graduates of the Polish school during
the 1950's were the Polish director Andrzej Munk and the
well known actor and director Roman Polanski. During the
late 1950's, the Prague Film Academy also increased its
reputation as a creative center for the arts and theory of
film-making. Its liberal atmosphere and the resulting innovative work of its graduates are now considered to be an
important part of the intellectual ferment that produced the
Dubcek regime of 1968. Together with the more traditionally
oriented Budapest school, the Lodz and Prague institutes
formed the basis for the sudden flowering of cinema in
Eastern Europe at the end of the 1950's.

Film institutes have been established in Rumania and
Bulgaria, but neither of these has the prestige of the older
film schools in Eastern Europe. Yugoslavia has no film
school, although cinema departments exist within the theatre
academies at Belgrade and Zagreb. Most of Yugoslavia's
professional film-makers still are enlisted from the legion
of amateur photographers and actors. They receive little
or no formal training. Albania, like Yugoslavia, offers little
or no formal education in the cinema and its techniques to
its few film-makers. To the Albanians, steeped in a varia-
tion of Maoist thought, the only appropriate training for a
film worker is found in making films.

Conclusions

Paul Babitsky, a former scenario writer in the Soviet
film studios, once described the Soviet studio as "a factory

that produces Bolshevik propaganda material." There are
several indications that the Communist Party of the Soviet
Union has tried to impart the characteristics of a factory to
their studios. The attempts to coordinate the movie industry with the rest of the economy, the support of technical
education in preparation for a film career and the attempts
to give the director's authority over production to studio
bureaucrats are all symptoms of the continuing effort to run
the film industry as if it were as rational as hydroelectric
dam construction. The Soviet Union is not alone in this effort; recently the relatively liberal Polish film industry condemned the "cult of the director" and demanded a return to
control of production by Party ideologues and studio bureaucrats.

        The effort to rationalize the film industry can never
be totally successful because, although the elements of film
are dependent on technology, film is also a highly creative
art. The film director is not simply a film studio foreman;
he is the artist whose personal style will decide whether a
motion picture will be a masterpiece or a bomb. Because
of this creative aspect and because of the sheer complexity
of film production, it is impossible to run a film studio like
a factory.

        The emphasis on propaganda content in the cinema,
insured by government censorship and Party supervision,
creates a problem similar to that engendered by the emphasis on industrial efficiency. As noted earlier, ideological
review of scenarios and films is extremely thorough, through
both the bureaucratic censorship procedures and the screening of studio personnel. In addition, directors may be successfully propagandized during their training at the film institutes. Nevertheless, the effectiveness of propaganda is
dependent on the film director's ability to insert the social
message into his work without alienating his audience. This
poses a major problem for the Soviet director: if he makes
the propaganda in his film too subtle, the Party censors will
disapprove and he will have to revise the film; but if he
makes the propaganda message too strident, he will lose the
attention of the audience. How this balancing act was accomplished during the comparatively liberal period prior to
1930 is the topic of the next chapter.

CHAPTER 2

CLASSIC COMMUNIST CINEMA, 1919-1929

On December 5th, 1926, the first Soviet film to be shown in the United States held its premiere at the Biltmore Theater in New York. No celebrity attended the first showing of Battle Cruiser Potemkin. The reviewer from the New York Times, Mordaunt Hall, saw little of lasting value in the film and spoke of the "few bits of real art" that the director, Sergei Eisenstein, incorporated into the propaganda. Hall found the reactions of the audience far more newsworthy than the film itself:

> Last night, it was apparent that the applause came from prejudiced persons, for the admirable features of the film passed without a murmur, while an officer being thrown into the sea, the rescue of the ringleaders of the insurrectionists and a title reading 'Down With the Czar!' stirred some spectators to a high pitch of enthusiasm.

In the late 1920's, when Eisenstein attempted to work in the United States, the propaganda element of his films rebounded against him. Before he could complete a single feature, he was blacklisted and a pamphlet damning him as a Bolshevik Jew circulated among film distributors, forcing his return to the U.S.S.R.

Today, Eisenstein is recognized as one of the great film directors and Potemkin is hailed as one of his greatest works. Moviegoers line up in front of theaters presenting his films, including the two silent, heavily propaganda-laden creations of his early years. The same reviewer who criticized Potemkin at its premiere later described Eisenstein as "the D. W. Griffith of the Russian screen." American photography students study his carefully arranged composition, a skill which he felt was essential for the success of his innovative editing technique. In short, divorced from

13

Fig. 1. Battleship Potemkin, the Odessa steps sequence. Courtesy, Museum of Modern Art.

the emotional propaganda messages of his work, Eisenstein
and his lesser colleagues of early Soviet cinema have "made
it" as artists in the eyes of world criticism.

And yet, earlier judgments of Eisenstein were partly
true. He and his Soviet contemporaries were undeniably
propagandists and, while modern critics are right to praise
the aesthetic qualities of their work, the early Russian directors were important in their own time and their own
country primarily for the political value of their creations.
Their importance lay in the Bolsheviks' desperate need for
propaganda.

Why Propaganda Was Necessary

Harold Lasswell defines the purpose of propaganda as
the influencing of attitudes among large numbers of people.
He qualifies this by distinguishing propaganda, which involves
controversial issues of importance to an interest group--
religious sect, political faction, economic entity--from education, which avoids controversial matters. Jacques Ellul,
in his work Propagandes, proposes that all governments in
a modern society must be, to some extent, propagandists.
It is his contention that the entry of a mass society into political action has created this necessity by forcing all governments to respond to public opinion. Since public opinion is
too vague to follow, according to Ellul, governments must
become opinion leaders, insuring that the "ever-present,
ponderous impassioned mass" is convinced that the government's decisions are legitimate and good.

In addition, Ellul maintains that every government,
acting under the belief that government operates by the con-
sent of the governed, tries to preserve at least an illusion
of legitimacy. He adds that the theory of the sovereignty of
the people--that power is legitimate only when it stems from
the will of the people--has become equally universal with the
spread of Western political ideologies. Whenever a portion
of the body of European political theory, whether liberal
democratic, Marxist or even fascist, is adopted as the ideology of a non-Western state, the basic principle of legitimacy is absorbed as well. Thus, to create the aura of
legitimacy, governments must prove themselves to be the
true expression of the people. This is accomplished through
such means as referendums, demonstrations, elections and
mass meetings. To guarantee the success of such proofs,

the mass population must be propagandized into believing that
the regime really does express their will.

It may be argued that the two reasons for propaganda--
the creation of an aura of legitimacy and of popular support
for the government programs--are invalid in a dictatorial
state such as the Soviet Union. After all, the Communist
Party of the Soviet Union (CPSU) has never made a bid for
broad support through mass membership. The Party leaders
could not claim to have been chosen by the Russian people.
On the contrary, the Constituent Assembly elected after the
October Revolution was mainly Social Democratic in composition and had to be forcibly dissolved on orders from Lenin
during its second meeting.

Until 1922, however, several non-Communist governments existed on Soviet soil that competed militarily and dip-
lomatically with the Bolsheviks for the mantle of legitimacy,
both at home and abroad. Following the defeat of the Whites
at the end of the Civil War, anti-Communist "governments-
in-exile" still functioned, demanding recognition. As late as
the early 1930's, the rulers of the Soviet Union feared a re-
currence of foreign military intervention on behalf of another
"legitimate" regime, meaning a regime claiming to be more
representative of the "real" will of the Russian people.
Thus, legitimacy was sought by the Communists as a weapon
against the claims of competing "Russian governments."

In addition to this pragmatic reason for establishing
an appearance of legitimacy, the orthodox Communists added
an ideological one. Government in the workers' state was
to be a "true" expression of the people's will, in direct contrast to the autocratic Tsarist regime and the "false" democ-
racies of the bourgeois West. For this reason, it was vital
for the Communists to demonstrate that they were the true
instruments of their subjects' desires, and this required, in
turn, that they establish an effective program of internal
propaganda.

The necessity for creating favorable public opinion in
order to govern effectively also existed for the early Soviet
Union, despite the very high centralization of decision making
in that country. Ideology dictated that the regime enact
sweeping social changes, changes which required the support
of the masses. The goals desired by the new regime--forced
industrialization, rural collectivization and the replacement
of the Orthodox Church with atheism--ran counter to the

traditional values of the majority of the Russian people. Against massive opposition, the authority of new laws and the apparatus of State terror would not have been enough to achieve these goals. Propaganda was necessary.

This need for favorable public opinion was particularly crucial during the first two decades of Communist rule when the material benefits of communism were not evident. The Communists, who had obtained power with the slogan "Peace and Bread," were unable to supply either for years after the October Revolution. War continued in the West for four years after the seizure of power, in Siberia for an additional year and in the frontiers of Central Asia for over a decade. Bread was not forthcoming after resistance to grain requisition policies and bad harvests brought grain supplies down to half the 1914 level. Even the industrial sphere suffered; production in 1921 was less than 20 percent of the 1916 level. The first meager benefits of the Revolution in terms of produced goods and adequate food did not appear until after the New Economic Policy had been established, and these benefits were, at best, poorly distributed.

When Josef Stalin achieved power in 1927, collectivization and forced industrialization were undertaken with greater ruthlessness than before. These projects met the same indifference and hostility among the population as the earlier attempts. Coercion in support of the new programs reached new levels of scope and brutality, but coercion alone was probably not able to insure more than mere acceptance of the programs, and the situation required an attitude different from mere acceptance.

The kind of attitude desired by the Communists was similar to that aimed for by wartime propaganda. Both in the early Soviet Union and in a state at war, the population had to be convinced that they should engage in what Ernest Kris and Nathan Leites describe as "social participation." By their definition, social participation is an attitude which includes concern for group goals, active involvement in group projects and willingness to undergo hardships on behalf of the group's welfare. High "social participation" is therefore synonymous with high morale.

It is clear why a social participation attitude is needed in wartime. A failure to involve the population in the defense of the homeland is fatal in a conflict with an enemy whose population is mobilized for aggression. In the case

of the early years of the Soviet Union, the enemy was the
backward condition of the Russian economy, the vestiges of
capitalism and, incidentally, the perceived threat of a foreign
invasion. Failure to develop the economy of the Soviet Union
would be a defeat for the regime, but the economy could be
transformed only with active support of the population, motivated by a high degree of social participation.

However, as indicated earlier, the majority of the
people of the Soviet Union were initially indifferent or hostile
to the goal of constructing a modern socialist economy. Nor
was the majority interested in sharing in the activities of
forced industrialization and collectivization demanded by the
ideological objective. "Social participation" was obviously
minimal. Stalinist coercion could not change the attitude of
the population; it could only modify behavior. Therefore,
an effective program of propaganda was necessary to create
a high level of social participation. Without it, the regime
could not achieve its ideological goals.

In summary, the Communists discovered that their
need to propagandize their subjects during the 1920's and
1930's was as great as or greater than the similar need
found within a democracy. This need was based on the regime's
desire for an aura of legitimacy and the necessity for a high
degree of social participation. Although both these demands
probably exist in milder forms under all types of government,
they were reinforced in the case of the early Soviet Union by
the dictates of Marxist-Leninist ideology. Thus, the survival of the regime was partly dependent on the success of
a blanket propaganda campaign in support of the goals of the
state.

Why Film Was Used

Much has been written on the techniques of early Soviet internal propaganda since the techniques were successful
in achieving desired results. The early propagandists demonstrated a high degree of ingenuity and imagination, as well
as a practical understanding of their subjects' psychology.
Perhaps we inhabitants of the electronic age can smile at the
image of truckloads of entertainers and Party spokesmen
driving through the wheatfields of the Ukraine, playing music
and urging the peasants to greater productivity, but these
naive techniques were effective enough. The desired result--
greater productivity--was attained.

Film-making, however, involves a higher level of sophistication and financial expenditure than other forms of propaganda. With a government beset with financial difficulties,
the expense of large-scale film production must have seemed
frivolous to many Party officials. Before the revolution, the
Bolsheviks had enjoyed great success with inexpensive, grass-
roots propaganda and street demonstrations. Why, then, did
the Soviet government begin large-scale film production and
financing as early as 1919, a period of economic collapse?

The answer lies in a combination of several factors,
chief of which was the size of the public which the Soviet
government was trying to influence. Before the October Revolution, the target public for Communist propaganda was essentially a few thousand factory workers in a few key cities,
university students, the sailors of the Kronstadt naval base,
and the soldiers concentrated in the front lines. It was relatively easy for a few hundred well trained agitators to propagandize these relatively few, highly concentrated groups.
Once power was achieved, however, the Bolsheviks were
faced with the task of communicating with and influencing a
population of 140 million, thinly distributed over eight million
square miles and speaking more than thirty separate languages. As Ellul states, propaganda in a mass society is
impossible without resorting to mass communication techniques. If this is true for Ellul's France, then it must have
been more emphatically true in a country with three times
the French population and only one-tenth the population den-
sity.

There exist only a few instruments of mass communication today, and fewer were available to the Communists in
the 1920's. Television, of course, was not yet invented and
radio, although developing rapidly as a device for international propaganda, required electricity and the mass distribution of radio receivers, neither of which the Soviet government could supply. Newspapers and periodicals were available and very useful, but as late as 1928, fully half of the
population of the Soviet Union was probably illiterate in the
Russian language. In addition to this drawback, writing and
printing were difficult to control effectively since the equipment for producing printed material is inexpensive and the
ability to read carries with it the ability to write. In effect,
every recipient of written propaganda became a potential
source of written counter-propaganda. Finally, the recipient
of written propaganda must be already motivated to read the
material before he can be reached by its message, and this

motivation was difficult to produce. It is possible that a majority of any population does not enjoy reading ... at least
not the polemical literature offered by the ruling regime.

Since radio and written propaganda presented difficulties for the propagandists, they turned to the use of film.
Film-making is a relatively expensive and technical activity
and is therefore relatively easy for a government to control,
as noted in the previous chapter. Films in the 1920's were
silent and thus transcended the language barrier. They did
not require any acquired skills, like literacy, on the part of
the audience. As with radio, the message content of a film
could reach a relatively large audience but, unlike radio, a
film projector required a power source no larger than a
portable generator. Films could be shown almost as readily
in a Siberian village as in downtown Moscow. Like printed
propaganda, each print of a film was a permanent record
but, unlike books and newspapers, film was still an attractive novelty. Film was the obvious solution to the problem
of propagandizing a vast, thinly-distributed audience in a pre-
electronic technology. It is, in fact, the same solution to
the identical problem that is being followed today by the government of India, making the Republic of India the world's
single largest producer of motion pictures.

Films not only solved the demographic problem of the
early Soviet propagandists but also proved to be more effective as an emotion-creating device than any other available
means. A highly gifted orator could, on occasion, rouse
the public of a limited area to enthusiastic support, but every
orator has his bad days when he is not as effective. A film
is equally effective at each performance. It enabled the public to participate in battles and events that occurred thousands
of miles away while allowing propagandists to change history
to favor their cause and enhance the emotional impact. In
portraying a demonstration, for example, a competent propaganda film director could ensure that the Tsarist police were
clearly brutal, sadistic and inhuman, while the Bolshevik
agitators could represent decency, humanity and populism.

Mordaunt Hall was incorrect in assuming that the
audience who cheered the Bolsheviks and hissed the Tsarists
at the premiere of Potemkin were necessarily prejudiced.
The audience was reacting predictably to the melodramatic
events depicted by Eisenstein, using the realism of the film
medium to enhance the emotional involvement. Only a motion
picture could produce this controlled, yet highly emotional

effect during the 1920's.   This is why Lenin stated, in 1921,
"Of all the arts, the cinema is most important to us. "

The Origins of Soviet Film

Cinema was not unknown in Russia before the October
Revolution, but it was slow in developing.   The aristocracy
enjoyed imported features, including those made on location
in Russia, but the native-produced product was technically
inferior and disdained by Russian audiences.

Two factors which were continued under the Communist regime appeared very early in Russian cinema: censorship and government sponsorship.   The Tsarist censorship of
the motion picture industry was typically inefficient and arbitrary.   A film which could be shown without interference in
a Moscow theater would be raided the next week for moral
or political reasons in Kiev.   In fairness to the Tsarist police, it must be admitted that the revolutionaries frequently
used movie theaters to their political advantage, often interrupting the performance to make a political speech under
cover of darkness.

Government sponsorship of the motion picture industry
first appeared in 1913, when several films were commissioned
to celebrate the tri-centennial of the Romanov dynasty.   During the First World War, the Skobelev Committee of the Ministry of the Interior drafted cameramen and directors to make
newsreels at the front.   Later, during the short-lived reign
of the Provisional Government, the Social Democrats commissioned anti-Tsarist, anti-Rasputin and, belatedly, anti-
Bolshevik motion pictures in an effort to discredit the opposition.

✶   During the Civil War that immediately followed the
October Revolution, no films were made in the Soviet Union
other than a few propaganda newsreels produced by Narkompros, the People's Commissariat of Education.   At this time,
Lenin established the principle known as the "Lenin proportion" in a directive to the Narkompros.   This principle established a definite ratio between the number of propaganda
films and the number of entertainment films to be produced
each year.   Although the Lenin proportion's definition of
"entertainment" was too vague for the principle to be put
into practice, it created a distinction in the minds of the
Party bureaucrats between films that conveyed a message

and films that were designed for amusement. This later had
serious consequences for the creativity of the motion picture
industry under Stalin.

A second part of Lenin's directive recommended the
establishment of more movie theaters "in the villages and in
the East, where they will be novelties and where, therefore,
our propaganda will be especially successful." This part of
the directive was followed, and distribution was placed under
government monopoly to limit the number of imported, bourgeois films seen by the Russian public in the new theaters.
Thus, the first successful Soviet controls of the motion picture industry were in the area of distribution.

Shortly after the establishment of the New Economic
Policy, the Council of People's Commissars, the forerunner
of the modern Council of Ministers, decreed the formation of
a stock company whose shareholders consisted of Narkompros
and the independent movie studios. This company, Sovkino,
dominated Soviet film-making throughout the 1920's. Gradually, the formerly independent studios and Sovkino merged
as the budgets of individual feature films exceeded the ca-
pacities of the local production companies. Twelve features
were produced in 1923, forty-one in 1924, and the rate of
production continued its increase during the next several
years. Sovkino worked closely at this time with the new
Moscow State Film Institute, then dominated by the brilliant
theorists V. E. Meyerhold and Lev Kuleshov. Their workshops produced a generation of directors and technicians of
unusual technical and artistic experience. Meyerhold himself
did not direct after the Revolution, and Kuleshov was responsible for only a handful of comparatively minor works--with
one exception--from 1919 until his death in 1970. Nevertheless, their ideas on editing, camerawork and design provided
the theoretical background for the creations of the great early
Soviet directors: Shub, Dovzhenko, Pudovkin and, the greatest
of the four, Eisenstein.

Eisenstein's Battle Cruiser Potemkin

One of the first films made during the Sovkino period
of Soviet film-making was Sergei Eisenstein's masterwork,
Potemkin. The film was shot in the fall of 1925, edited by
Eisenstein himself in December and released on January 16th.
It was re-edited almost immediately afterwards for showing
abroad, a tribute to its unusual appeal and quality. It

remains the most famous work of the director.

Sergei Mikhailovich Eisenstein was not a Russian, but he was very definitely a Bolshevik. Born into a Jewish Latvian family in 1898, he was barely old enough to officially join the Party and enlist in the Red Army when the October Revolution erupted. For the next two years, he was a fortifications engineer on the Ukrainian front, but much of his time was spent organizing an amateur theater group among the soldiers of his command. After his discharge, he drifted to Moscow, where he became a director of mass spectacles and open-air dramas for the Narkompros. Later, he studied under Meyerhold at the Moscow State Film Institute. His first film, Strike!, was released in the spring of 1925, but was poorly received by the Russian audiences. Even before Strike! was completed, he had volunteered for a commission from Sovkino to direct a feature celebrating the twentieth anniversary of the abortive Russian Revolution of 1905. This Commission eventually resulted in the film Battle Cruiser Potemkin.

The story of Battle Cruiser Potemkin is based on the historical mutiny on board the cruiser "Prince Potemkin Tavrichevsky" in July of 1905. Since Eisenstein himself was only six years old at the time of the mutiny, he must have received the story second-hand, but his sources are unknown. Parts of the film correspond to the historical events. The real mutiny began with a protest over rotten meat being used in the ship's mess, as is described in the film. A sailor named Matyushenko organized the sailors who seized control of the ship, murdering the officers. When the mutinous warship landed at the port of Odessa, people from the city supplied the rebels with food, as Eisenstein depicted. Later, also as in the film, the "Prince Potemkin" sailed through a squadron of intercepting loyalist ships without a shot being fired.

There was a natural atmosphere of drama and suspense in the incident which any good director could recognize. Eisenstein, however, was not content with a newsreel-style reenactment of the mutiny. He wanted the mutiny to be accepted by his audience as part of something far greater, something which the audience was also involved in: the struggle for socialism. This is where his creative genius entered into the film, enhancing its propaganda value.

One idea which Eisenstein wished to emphasize in

Potemkin was the collective hero. This was to be a radical innovation in drama in which the mass was to be seen as the protagonist, instead of just one or two leading actors. It was possible only through the use of the film medium, since space limitation prevented the collective hero from being represented on stage. The use of the collective hero was an experiment in cinematic technique that was perfectly adaptable to the propaganda version of the 1905 Revolution which was being promoted by the Soviet government in the 1920's.

By portraying the Russian people as the hero of the 1905 Revolution, particularly of the "Potemkin" mutiny incident, Eisenstein believed that his audience would readily identify with the successful Bolshevik October Revolution and sympathize with the aims of the Communist revolutionaries. Although the 1905 Revolution was later depicted by the Communist Party as the brainchild of an omnipotent Lenin, the propaganda of the pre-Stalin era depicted both the 1905 and 1917 revolutions as spontaneous movements of the enraged Russian proletariat. Thus, Eisenstein's interpretation of the "Potemkin" mutiny fit that of the Party.

Only four experienced actors played roles in Potemkin. Of these, two played leaders of the mutiny while the others played a pair of villainous Tsarist naval officers. It was the task of these four actors to initiate the theme on a personal level of individuals matched against individuals. This conflict later evolves to the higher level of the heroic revolutionary mass of the Russian people matched against the mass power of the tyrannical Tsarist regime. The other individual roles in the film were performed by such people as "an anonymous workman" who played the role of the Ship Surgeon, Smirnov, and "an anonymous old gardener from the orchards on the outskirts of Sevastopol" who portrayed a priest. The remaining actors were grouped under the three categories of sailors of the Red Navy, assorted citizens of Odessa and the apprentices of the Protekult Theater.

The first people seen in the film are the two sailors, Matyushenko and Vakulinchuk, who briefly speak together in a conspiratorial manner, establishing the fact that they are the revolutionaries. Immediately afterwards, the audience is introduced to the first Tsarist, anti-revolutionary character:

A fat boatswain with a brutal face descends

            the ladder into the lower deck and looks
            with malice at
            ... the sleeping sailors.

The boatswain reinforces the "villain" image by spitefully
lashing the back of a young, sleeping sailor with a convenient chain. At this point, attention is shifted back to
Vakulinchuk, exhorting the sailors to revolt, not for the
cause of socialism but because "All Russia has arisen,"
according to the title. These three scenes serve to identify
individuals and establish early hero/villain relationships.
They are very conventional episodes, characteristic of silent
screen drama prior to Eisenstein's innovations.

      The next episode enlarges the scope of conflict. A
confrontation appears between a group of sailors, Vakulinchuk
among them, and two officers: Smirnov the surgeon, "a
small, short-sighted man, his courage comically mustered,"
and Senior Officer Gilyarovsky, "a malicious, fierce-faced
officer." The source of the dispute is a maggoty side of
beef which the officers insist is fit for consumption by the
men, a contention angrily denied by Vakulinchuk and the
other sailors. Vakulinchuk, although already identified as
an individual hero, has only a few short lines in this scene.
He does not play the part of a leader, but merely acts as
spokesman for the small group of men, working together as
a unit. The silly surgeon and the bullying Gilyarovsky, acting as individuals, are contrasted against this collective
solidarity. At this point in the story, the conflict is between
a small-scale collective hero--the sailors as a group--and
two individual villains, later joined by the villainous boatswain.

      Throughout the mutiny which follows, the conflict re-
mains primarily on the level of individual officers fighting
against groups of angry sailors. Again, however, there is
an enlargement of scope as it becomes apparent that the
whole crew is rebelling against the entire officer corps of
the "Potemkin." The rebellion is expressed in terms of
local incidents, filmed anecdotes of the mutiny: a single
officer standing on the wardroom piano firing his revolver
into a crowd of unarmed sailors; the cowardly Smirnov
hiding from a group of sailors, then tossed by them into the
sea; an officer running through the ship's kitchen, fleeing
a group of pursuers.

      Gilyarovsky, the single most important villain, and

Vakulinchuk, the most important individual hero, do not participate in the mass actions of the mutiny. Instead, the sol-
itary officer, armed with a rifle, chases the unarmed sailor,
occasionally struggling with him. Ultimately, the officer
shoots Vakulinchuk, killing him.

Meanwhile, the crew, without the leadership of
Vakulinchuk, has successfully seized control of the "Potemkin." Gilyarovsky disappears from the action after the murder and the film proceeds from this point to its conclusion
without individual heroes and villains. The remaining conflicts are intergroup rather than interpersonal. Thus, half-
way through the film, Eisenstein has achieved the creation
of the collective hero by advancing in stages from the strictly
interpersonal conflict between the boatswain and the sleeping
sailor, through the individual-group conflict of Gilyarovsky
and Smirnov against the sailors, to the mutiny itself, where
the intergroup clash between the ship's company and the officers is reflected in the isolated personal conflict between
Vakulinchuk and Gilyarovsky.

The most famous scenes of the film, the Odessa steps
sequences, are the triumph of Eisenstein's emphasis on the
collective hero and his use of montage. In this segment of
the work, the action centers upon a large crowd of Odessa
citizens mourning Vakulinchuk, cheering the sailors, and supplying food to the rebel warship. These actions were not
depicted in the style of D. W. Griffith, with vast mobs of
"extras" continually milling around the set. Instead, Eisenstein alternated between shots of the whole crowd and close-
ups of individuals within the crowd. A glimpse of a student
agitator is juxtaposed with a shot of the entire crowd of
which he is a part; a college professor and his family are
placed in contrast with the fleet of graceful sailboats supplying the "Potemkin"; a poor woman with a shawl, a legless
invalid and a woman with a lorgnette and veil are all identified within the excited mass of spectators lining the harbor
quay, cheering as the red flag is raised over the revolutionary battleship.

The montage technique has the effect of transforming
the crowd on the Odessa quay into something more than a
crowd at a particular event in a specific time and place.
Instead, the crowd is carefully chosen to be a representative
spectrum of the entire Russian people. The audience in the
theater seeing Potemkin could easily identify with the people
on the quay, since the spectators, like the theater audience,

were a homogeneous sampling of Russians viewing the events
on the warship.

Having created this emotional rapport between the
citizens of Odessa and the audience, Eisenstein proceeded to
exploit it.   He wished to direct the emotion he had created
into horror and anger directed against the old regime.   To
accomplish this, he used what he later described as "shock
effect."   The scenes of the cheering people are cut short by
a title reading, "Suddenly ..."   A unit of Tsarist infantry
and a brigade of Cossack cavalry charge the people in the
waterfront area and the crowd flees in terror.

The conflict has now been extended to its highest
level: the vast "collective hero" of the citizens of Odessa are
brutally attacked by the awesome "collective villain" of dehumanized Tsarist soldiers.   Not content with depicting the
massacre from afar, Eisenstein again closes his camera in
to reveal separate individual horrors within the mass tragedy,
as outlined in his script:

> The legs of the soldiers move on.
> A beautiful woman shields a baby carriage
> containing a child from the fleeing people.
> Relentless, like a machine, the rank of
> soldiers descends the steps.
> The beautiful woman opens her mouth in terror.
> ... and clings to the side of the carriage.
> With her body, she shields the child in the
> carriage from the fleeing people
> The rank of soldiers descends the steps
> ... and fires.
> In terrible pain, the mother throws back her
> head.
> The carriage with the child comes to rest at
> the edge of the steps ...
> The rank of soldiers fires into the crowd.
> The student shouts in terror.
> The carriage with the child overturns.
> A cossack brandishes
> ... his sword
> ... and puts out the eye of the elderly
> woman in the pince-nez.

Through quick-cutting techniques, Eisenstein kept the
action moving at lightning pace, causing the eye to be drawn
from one horror to the next.   In the end, the audience is

left with the feeling of collective suffering and collective tragedy that Eisenstein wished to create.

What did Eisenstein accomplish through the use of the
collective hero? First, he had achieved absolute audience
identification with the group that supported the revolutionary
sailors. This alone was a major propaganda victory since
it caused the audience to identify themselves with the revolution. Secondly, through the principle that an emotional crowd
scene will infect its onlookers with emotion, he brought the
theater audience to an emotional peak. Finally, through the
use of montage and "shock effect," he skillfully directed this
emotion into a feeling of horror and anger against the tyran-
nies of the old regime.

The problem remained for Eisenstein to use the audience's heightened identification with the revolutionaries to the
best possible propaganda advantage. I have already mentioned
that the spectators in the waterfront sequence cheered the
raising of the red flag. Later, as the rebel ship passes
through the squadron of loyalist vessels, the sailors on the
Tsarist warships also cheer the sight of the red flag. Since
the red flag had been adopted as the symbol of the Bolsheviks,
Eisenstein was able to transfer the sympathy of the audience
from the revolutionary sailors of 1905 to the ruling former
revolutionaries of 1925. It was probable that after the early
presentations of Potemkin in the provinces, a speaker would
appear in front of the screen to underscore this point with
an emotional harangue. This is known to have been the practice during screenings of the film at Communist meetings in
the West.

The part of the Bolshevik program that was most difficult for the peasants to accept, after collectivization of farm-
land, was the anti-religious campaign. Anti-religious propaganda in Potemkin is limited to a few scattered incidents.
Eisenstein wisely chose to direct the propaganda towards
anti-clericalism, since it was the clergy that was the true
enemy of the regime, not religion. The only member of the
clergy seen in Potemkin is the priest on the warship, who
first appears when a group of rebellious sailors are covered
by a tarpaulin prior to execution:

> The ship's priest comes on deck and raises
> his hand to the sky.
> 'Lord, let these sinners understand.'
> Some of the sailors covered with tarpaulin

> fall to their knees.
> The priest raises his cross and speaks.
> Senior Officer Gilyarovsky orders:
> 'At the tarpaulin ... aim!'

The clergy is represented by an unkempt, bearded, wild-eyed old man, played by the "anonymous old gardener." He appears for the last time during the fight scene between Vakulinchuk and Gilyarovsky, again working on the side of the Tsarist cause:

> From the hatch appears the figure of the
> priest, cross in hand, ascending the ladder.
> Vakulinchuk looks at him uncomprehendingly.
> The priest speaks to him,
> 'Fear God!'
> ... and stretches out the cross to him.
> Vakulinchuk shouts at the priest:
> 'Get out of the way, you sorcerer!'

Through the priest's action, Gilyarovsky is able to obtain the rifle with which he later kills Vakulinchuk.

Despite the anti-clericalism, the funeral of Vakulinchuk is pointedly portrayed in the traditional Russian Orthodox manner with candles and offerings before the altar. Through this minor subterfuge, Eisenstein was able to follow the current anti-religious line of propaganda without risking the alienation of the strongly Russian Orthodox peasant audiences.

The genius of Eisenstein was his combination of effective propaganda with brilliantly creative film artistry, both in content and stylistic features. Not every one who saw Potemkin in the West during the 1920's agreed with Mordaunt Hall's short-sighted criticism. Douglas Fairbanks, who first saw the film on a European tour, reportedly described it as "the greatest motion picture ever made." The High Command of the Army of the Weimar Republic thought Potemkin so effective that they forcibly prevented their soldiers from seeing it, for fear of a Communist mutiny. An anonymous editorial writer for the New York Times (the same paper that contained Mordaunt Hall's review) compared it favorably to the contemporary Hollywood product:

> It is but fair to concede it is propaganda
> only as impartial journalism may be. In this
> instance, the Soviets have not materially

tampered with the facts. 'Armored Cruiser
Potemkin' is journalism in films--a record of
what actually happened when the crew of the
cruiser mutinied off Odessa in June, 1905.

The result is more contemporary and
convincing than it could have been by an
introduction of 'what the public wants' ...
Aided by artistic photography, the film carries
with it a weight of conviction, a lesson in
human solidarity, far more dramatic than
anything within the ken of close-ups of the Red
flag or flaming subtitles. If this be
propaganda, let Hollywood imitate it.

Of course, the editorial writer was dead wrong. In
the first place, there were close-ups of the Red flag and
flaming subtitles incorporated into the film, but they were
incorporated so skillfully that the viewer did not identify
them as propaganda devices. Secondly, Potemkin is far
from impartial journalism. The massacre on the Odessa
steps, for example, is a complete fabrication with no basis
in history. In any event, no dramatization can be an impartial record of "what actually happened." However, the
writer was correct in observing that Potemkin is a work of
convincing realism. It has the look of a newsreel of what
might have happened, but is far more valuable as propaganda
than the historical events could have been. An objective
newsreel might have found some heroism displayed by the
Tsarist officers or some sadistic cruelty on the part of the
mutineers; while this might have added to the realism it
might also have detracted from the social message of the
film. As Eisenstein conceived it, Battle Cruiser Potemkin
transformed the mutiny into part of the grand, continuing
struggle of the Russian people towards socialism, a complete
distortion of the event on behalf of the regime. This combination of artistic quality and ideological effectiveness was
not achieved again by a Soviet director for another decade.

Sergei Eisenstein apparently retained his pragmatic
Bolshevik ideological viewpoint. Unfortunately for his career,
the Soviet government did not. As early as 1927, the Communist Party censored Ten Days that Shook the World, Eisenstein's documentary on the October Revolution, because some
of the scenes depicted Trotsky, who was already being edited
out of Soviet history. As Stalin consolidated his power and
changed the ideological line to suit his purposes, Eisenstein

fell into disrepute. Although he began several films after
1927 (The General Line, Bezhin Meadow), he was not permitted to complete any of them. In each case, their propaganda was at variance with the official ideology of the early
Stalinist period. Eisenstein faded into the background, attempting to work abroad and teaching at the Moscow State
Film Institute. In effect, he was retired from active film-
making at the age of 32, while rival directors replaced him
at the Sovkino studios. The most important of these was
Vsevolod Ilarionovich Pudovkin.

Pudovkin's "Storm over Asia"

        V. I. Pudovkin was born in Moscow in 1893 and did
not begin to work in dramatics until three years after the
October Revolution. From 1916 until 1920 he was a prisoner
of war in Germany. After his release, he returned to Moscow to find his former home destroyed, his family scattered
and his hopes of renewing his studies in chemistry at Moscow University totally futile. There is a story which claims
that Pudovkin decided to become an actor after seeing D. W.
Griffith's spectacle, Intolerance, at a Moscow theater.
Whether or not this is true, it is known that he enrolled as
a student of acting at the Moscow State Film Institute, quickly
becoming a member of Lev Kuleshov's workshop. Kuleshov
made him his protégé, giving him writing, directing and acting assignments in two of his early films. Pudovkin was an
immediate success. The detective thriller, The Death Ray,
in which Pudovkin played the leading role and wrote the
scenario, was released at the same time as Eisenstein's
Strike!, attracting tremendous crowds while Eisenstein's
work went almost unnoticed. That year of 1925 set the pattern for the success of the two men: the innovative Eisenstein fluctuated throughout his life between acclaim and dis-
grace, while the more pedestrian Pudovkin enjoyed a consistently large following and a benign acceptance by the Party
officials.

        Storm over Asia was Pudovkin's second feature film.
His first, based on a novel by Maxim Gorki, was as popular
as The Death Ray, but it was his scenario-writer, Natan
Zarkhi, who received the official credit for the film's success.

        Natan Zarkhi was catapulted to notoriety within the
Soviet film world by his creation of the accepted "formula"

for Soviet scenario writing:

> I strive to build a scenario on the basis of
> great dramatic conflicts, combining conflicts of
> social significance, such as wars, strikes and
> revolutions, with a conflict within the life of
> an individual. The socially significant event
> is then depicted as the turning point in the
> development of the individual and as responsible
> for the adoption of a new way of life.

This technique had been used before in literature, as in the
novels Germinal and War and Peace, but Zarkhi's formula
represented a change of emphasis. In earlier literary works,
the emphasis was on the internal development of the protagonist against a background of social upheaval. In Zarkhi's
formula, the emphasis is on humanizing the event. For example, the reconstruction of the economy is expressed in
this style of scenario writing in terms of the personal struggles of a dam engineer in defeating saboteurs and completing
his project on time, reducing the "conflict of social significance" to the personal level. The focus, however, remains
on the larger event rather than the personal drama of the
individual.

Storm over Asia shows the early influence of Zarkhi's
theories. Pudovkin chose the story of a Mongolian fur trapper during the Civil War, knowing the attraction of the exotic
East for the audiences in urbanized European Russia. At the
same time, the problems encountered by Pudovkin's hero
were chosen to be those familiar to the audience. The purpose of the fur trapper was to personalize the conflict between the Communist Reds and the villainous anti-Communist
Whites.

The exotic atmosphere of the film is established during the opening scene: a fair in the Mongolian "metropolis"
of Urga. The camera moves quickly among strange Asiatic
faces and costumes, fierce horsemen and Mongolian warriors
dressed in animal pelts. The characters, although exotic,
have a familiarity to Russian audiences acquainted with the
national tradition of Batu Khan's Mongol conquerors and their
reign in Russia, similar to America's "Old West" tradition.

The camera finally focuses in on the hero who, beam-
ing cheerfully with pride, is selling a beautiful silver fox
skin to a swarthy, shifty-looking European. The fur buyer

refuses to pay a fair price for the furs and the trapper stalks off angrily, with only a few coins in payment. Capitalism is thus condemned and the outraged trapper chooses the Communist cause, enlisting in the Red Army.

Pudovkin has not offered any great ideological arguments with flashing titles and socialist slogans or the hackneyed story of oppressed proletarians, dear to the heart of second-rate Communist propagandists. None of these tactics were readily accepted by the peasant audiences. Instead, Pudovkin reduced the complex economic issues to a simple, familiar level: under capitalism, a man did not always receive a fair wage for his work. What this statement lacks in sophistication, it gains in clarity and simplicity.

By joining the Red Army, the fur trapper is transformed into a Soviet superman. In battle, he is disarmed, but continues to fight on against heavy odds, finally being captured with difficulty by five or six White soldiers. Sentenced to be executed, the trapper manages to survive the firing squad. When his papers are discovered to indicate that he is the descendant of the legendary Genghis Khan, the Whites decide to make him a symbol for their cause. The fur trapper, however, refuses to remain passive and rebels, despite the wealth and honors lavished upon him by the Whites. Once again, his life is endangered, but he is saved again, partly through his own heroism and partly through the sudden arrival of Red Army cavalry at the last possible moment. This ending, of course, is strongly reminiscent of American "westerns" and it comes as no great surprise to discover that Pudovkin frequently expressed his admiration for the Hollywood product.

The American "western" establishes its hero/villain relationship through physical clues such as the color of the character's hat, how close the character shaved--five o'clock shadow was an almost sure sign of evil--and whether or not the character sang to his horse. Pudovkin did not have these well established means for depicting the hero and villain, but there was a certain amount of type-casting and Pudovkin used it to the best advantage. The fur trapper was portrayed by a popular actor of the period, Viktor Inkizhinov. The reactionary officers were directed to look haughty and pompous, while the genealogist who discovers the fur trapper's ancestry is a "mad doctor" stereotype. The wife of the reactionary British colonel bears a striking resemblance to Margaret Dumont, the dignified society woman who was the butt of the

Marx Brothers in several of their films.

In general, however, Pudovkin had to identify his
heroes and villains through their actions. The Communists
had to act noble and humble, non-Communists had to appear
craven and pompous. This was accomplished through anecdotal glimpses of character, as illustrated in one sequence
centering on a puddle in the middle of a dirt road. The fur
trapper, condemned to death by the Whites, and his British
guard are marching together to the firing squad when they
come to the puddle blocking the path. The fur trapper re-
solutely splashes through the puddle, while his enemy fastid-
iously circles around it. After the execution, the soldier is
visibly regretful and, returning alone to headquarters, he
angrily splashes through the same puddle, a convert to humanity.

A large amount of detail in the film is concerned with
displaying the foolishness and extravagance of bourgeois life.
One sequence juxtaposes the British colonel and his wife
dressing for a State banquet, with a group of Mongolian folk
dancers decorating themselves in barbaric costumes. Another
scene depicts the valet of the White District Commander
forced to polish the boots of the commander's empty uniform,
a hollow shell of military elegance without a touch of humanity
in it. Ultimately, there is the fur trapper himself, dressed
by the Whites as the head-of-state for their puppet regime,
looking as absurd in a tuxedo as he was heroic in his native
costume.

Analyzing these propaganda touches gives the false impression that the final effect of the film was contrived. In
reality, the propaganda technique employed by Pudovkin in
Storm over Asia is not nearly as complex or contrived as
extensive analysis may cause it to appear. The director's
attention to minute detail is an attempt to create audience
sympathy for his trapper-turned-Bolshevik in the struggles
with the Whites. Through this personal conflict, he works
to create sympathy for the Red cause as a whole. The basic
logic of this technique is absurd, but effective: since all the
heroes in the film are Communist and the villains are cari-
catured Whites, then all Communists must be the "good guys"
and Whites and foreign interventionists must be the "bad
guys." The rural Russian audience could identify with the
familiar smiling face of the fur trapper and feel resentment
against the alien, aristocratic officers of the opposition.
Thus, Pudovkin is using the process of "identification" on

two levels: first, to identify the audience with the hero, and
secondly, to identify the hero with the Bolsheviks.

It is difficult to judge whether or not this propaganda
technique was as effective as Eisenstein's innovative use of
the collective hero. The regime changed the classification
of the film haphazardly from entertainment to propaganda, to
entertainment again, in the course of only a few years. Apparently, the Party was uncertain as to the value of its sim-
plistic social message. Storm over Asia has been, at least,
a very popular motion picture, both in the USSR and abroad.
It stands as a monument to Pudovkin's knowledge of mass
taste, if not to his skill as a propagandist.

Ermler's Paris Shoemaker

Frederich Markovich Ermler was born in the same
city as Sergei Eisenstein, the same year and of similar
Jewish Latvian family background. They both joined the
Communist Party shortly after the October Revolution. At
this point, however, the superficial similarities end. In
1919, Eisenstein was in the Red Army, seeking glory on the
Ukrainian Front. At that time, Ermler was reportedly a
member of the Leningrad branch of the Cheka--the secret
police. The difference between the early careers of the two
men underscores their basic intellectual difference. Eisenstein was a maverick Communist, intent on combining his
artistic innovations with his very personal interpretations of
Marxism. Ermler, on the other hand, was always a Party
man first and a creative director second. For this reason,
Ermler was destined to become one of the most favored directors in the post-NEP period of the Soviet Union.

Ermler entered the Leningrad Institute of Motion Picture Arts in 1922, shortly after this inferior sister of the
Moscow State Film Institute was founded. As a student, his
main interest was acting; the debates on editing and design
which engrossed the students in Moscow did not exist in
Leningrad. After his graduation, in 1925, his work as a
director continued to focus on the manipulation of the actors,
ensuring that his characters displayed clearly defined, ideologically acceptable personalities. This approach was very
different from both Eisenstein's concept of the collective hero
and Pudovkin's use of his characters as larger-than-life symbols of revolutionary good and counter-revolutionary evil.

Paris Shoemaker, Ermler's fourth work, is one of
the few Soviet films produced to fill a specific need of the
Communist Party. In 1927, the Party echelons were becoming dismayed over the behavior of many members of Kom-
somol--the Young Communist League. A large percentage
of Communist youth had decided that the success of the Revolution meant an end to pre-revolutionary morality. They
practiced free love, derided marriage as outmoded and used
their newly won positions in government and the economy to
further their personal ambitions. The rest of the Party,
under the stern direction of Party Secretary Josef Stalin,
wanted to disassociate itself from the Komsomol "hooligans"
and hold their behavior up to public censure. As part of
the anti-hooligan campaign, the Party decided to order a
feature film which would express its feelings toward the
rebellious youth. This is why Paris Shoemaker, a strongly
anti-Komsomol film, was made.

Frederich Ermler was chosen to direct the film for
a variety of reasons. First, and most important, he was
known to be politically reliable. In terms of ideological content, he would portray what he was asked to portray. Secondly, although he did not have a reputation, his earlier
three films were sufficient evidence of his abilities as a
film-maker. Ermler was still relatively young, 29 years
old, and it was hoped that he could involve himself with the
youth problem more readily than an older man. Finally,
Ermler was known to be ambitious, and Paris Shoemaker
was a perfect vehicle to test a rising young director. If he
succeeded, he would greatly increase his standing in the
Party. If he failed, if he implicated the entire Party membership while portraying the immorality of the Komsomol
members, then the Party would know that he was not to be
trusted with such tasks in the future.

With these considerations in mind, Ermler took his
film crews to a small town in southern Russia. He chose
a "small town" setting in order to imply that the immoral
behavior of the Komsomol members was occurring in the
provinces, not in the cities. He began the film with a love
story between two Komsomol members, Katya and Andrei,
and deliberately uses a romantic atmosphere in order to win
approval for their love. Their neighbors, suspicious and
gossipy, are the initial villains.

The romantic mood ends abruptly when Katya tells
her lover that she is pregnant. At this point, the character

of Andrei begins a subtle transformation. He realizes that
he does not want the responsibility of a child; at first he is
confused and goes to the secretary of the Komsomol for advice. The secretary, although well meaning, cannot offer
any suggestions, so Andrei is forced to turn to his friends
for advice. Ermler has a grand time depicting these loafers
and n'er-do-wells hanging around the streets of the town.
Clearly non-Party members, they supply Andrei with a plan
to free himself of the responsibility for Katya; he must
force Katya to be seen with other people so that the towns-
people will not be certain who the father of Katya's child is.

     The plan works, but has consequences far worse than
Katya or Andrei anticipated. Katya's father, pressured by
the ever-present neighbors, throws Katya out of her house
and Andrei abandons her completely. Fortunately, a group
of "good" Komsomol members from Katya's factory bring
her to the shop of Kirik, a deaf-mute shoemaker who has
loved her from afar for years. Kirik eventually explains,
through gestures, that he knows the entire story and that
Andrei had forced her to behave immorally. Katya is reha-
bilitated through work at a collective, the depraved Andrei
is outcast from the community and the film ends with the
title--"Who is to be blamed here?" The answer, of course,
is Andrei.

     In some respects, Paris Shoemaker is a remarkable
film. Contemporary critics describe the actor who played
the role of Kirik, Feodor M. Nikitin, as a Soviet Chaplin.
The other performances, although not approaching Nikitin's,
were unusually good for the period. Ermler was successful
in creating an ideologically important drama which centered
on realistic people and human situations rather than on the
grandiose. He was also successful in portraying the decadence of some Komsomol members without indicting the entire organization--it was, after all, Komsomol members who
helped Katya after she was forced to leave home. Paris
Shoemaker brought Ermler the position in the film industry
which he was seeking; for the next ten years, he was prac-
tically the "official" film director of the Communist Party.

     On the other hand, Ermler's work can be criticized
for retaining too much of bourgeois soap-opera in its story.
This cannot be attributed solely to Ermler, since he did not
write the scenario for Paris Shoemaker. However, Ermler
used the melodramatic moments of the story to their most
tearful advantage. Aside from the acting and the use of the

town as a setting, <u>Paris Shoemaker</u> could have been a typical Hollywood melodrama. During the 1930's, it was withdrawn from distribution within the Soviet Union, partly because of its Western spirit. The more important reason for its with- drawal was the success of the early Party purges in elimi- nating the more frivolous Komsomol members, including those who had joined for the "wrong" reasons. There was no need, after the first purges, to imply that the purified Komsomol apparatus had ever been composed of any mem- bers besides dedicated young Communists.

The Decline of the Classic Soviet Film

         The winter of 1928-29 saw the creation of a new in- stitution in Soviet film-making: the Main Administration on Affairs in Art and Literature, a special governmental depart- ment for "ideological leadership" in the arts. In reality, this agency exercised stringent censorship on the propaganda of books, paintings, musical works and, above all, motion pictures. Unfortunately, positions of responsibility in the department did not go to either artists or propaganda spe- cialists. These positions tended to be handed over to per- sonal friends of Stalin as a reward for loyalty during the previous five years of struggle for Party control. Under the influence of the Lenin proportion, Party censors limited the content of "entertainment" films to very frivolous works or adaptations of approved Russian classics. At the same time, the new policies permitted film studios to produce scores of propaganda films whose entertainment value--and persuasive effect--was virtually nil.

         A second factor in the sudden decline of the quality of Soviet films during the late 1920's was the overbearing censorship of motion picture script writers, leading to a scenario shortage. As early as 1927, a third of the produc- tions in various stages of completion were cancelled for ideo- logical reasons. Some of these were replaced by scenarios written by amateurs, workers turned authors, with highly un- satisfactory results. Other cancelled films were not replaced with any productions. Rather than attempt to follow contin- ually shifting, arbitrary changes in propaganda content dic- tated by the Main Administration, the professional writers and directors fled from the film studios to work in media-- such as the legitimate theater--which were less tightly con- trolled. Other film-makers, like Eisenstein, attempted to work abroad or retreated into teaching positions. Still

others, like Pudovkin and Ermler, remained active by surrendering all creativity and working as closely as possible
with the Party officials.

   The combined effects of the Lenin proportion's misuse
and inept censorship put an end to the brief era of "classic"
Soviet film-making. By surrendering quality and creativity
to the confusing ideology of the early Stalinist years, the
Soviet cinema became a target for the artistic "guidance" of
the socialist realism movement.

CHAPTER 3

NATIONALIST CINEMA IN EASTERN EUROPE, 1908-1945

In the fall of 1908, the coffeehouses of Budapest were beginning to suffer loss of trade because of an innovation at the Café Venice. Two or three times each afternoon, the curtains of the Café Venice were drawn, the lights dimmed, and the murmur of German and Hungarian voices stilled as the head waiter hung a clean white sheet against the back wall. For the next twenty minutes, the Café Venice was transformed into Budapest's first movie theater. The films themselves--slapstick comedies, five-minutes of circus acts, occasional newsreels--were unimpressive, but Herr Ungerleider, the owner, didn't object. If the patrons ordered coffee during the program or used the darkness to take liberties with lady friends, the result was still good for business. Nevertheless, despite the mediocre content of the programs, most of the customers actually came to see the films and stayed to critique them. Among the regular clientele was the group of rebellious young intellectuals who were to dominate Hungarian film-making for the next decade and leave a lasting impact on world cinema.

In the other provinces of the Hapsburg Empire, the advent of cinema followed a similar pattern. In Kolozsvar (now Cluj), Prague, Vienna and Agram (now Zagreb), the motion picture began its existence as a primarily middle-class art form. As a result, early film-making in Danubian Europe reflected the tastes and values of the bourgeoisie. The censorship that had already appeared in Tsarist Russia was absent under the Hapsburgs. Perhaps because of this difference, the cinema in Eastern Europe attracted considerably more attention among the intellectuals of the region at an earlier stage of development than it did in Russia. Thus, Eastern European film before the First World War was already a unique combination of middle-class and intellectual aesthetic traditions.

False Dawn, 1908-1919

It is impossible to say in which of the countries of
Eastern Europe film-making first appeared as an industry.
Local entrepreneurs, actors, and camera enthusiasts throughout the region attempted to set up movie studios with varying
degrees of success. By 1912, the A-B Studios in Prague
and the vast Hunnia Studios in Budapest seemed to be on the
verge of feature film production, but their financial strength
turned out to be only a facade. By 1914, the A-B Studios,
faced with the problems of German competition and extremely
inferior equipment, was teetering on the edge of bankruptcy.
Hunnia had already given up the ghost. The main legacy of
the Hungarian experiment was the absurdly large vacant studio
complex in the suburbs of the capital which has since been
the property of successive Hungarian governments, including
the present one.

A major obstacle to film-making industries throughout
the silent film era was the monopolies established by the
local film distributors. The most powerful of these was
Projectograph, a firm founded by the former cafe owner,
Mors Ungerleider. Projectograph's almost total lack of competition within Hungary and Ungerleider's personal preference
for French and American films prevented those Hungarian intellectuals who were trying to create a national film industry
from selling their productions within Hungary. There were
frequent attempts to break the Projectograph monopoly from
1912 until 1914 and from 1919 until 1929. Each time, however, the attempts were doomed to failure. Very few theater
owners were willing to risk incurring Projectograph's wrath
by booking a film not offered to them by the monopoly. Similar situations, although not nearly as serious, existed in the
regions which were to become Poland, Czechoslovakia and
Croatia.

The First World War brought new life to the failing
motion picture industries of Eastern Europe. The Allied
blockade prevented new American and French films, formerly
the main programs of Eastern European theaters, from reaching the Austro-Hungarian Empire. Projectograph and the
other monopolistic distributors were temporarily forced to
rely on local producers to supply them with new films. This
pressure-cooker environment enabled the intellectuals who
had been attacking the distributors for favoring foreign films
to indulge in a brief flurry of domestic film-making. Alexander Korda, whose film-making technique during this period

is described in Chapter 1, shifted his operations from Budapest to Kolozsvar in Transylvania in 1916.   For the next two
years, the former film critic produced a record seven features per year for the Transylvanian Film Company.   Similar film-making "booms" appeared in Vienna and Prague.
Writers, actors, and businessmen, people who had never set
foot on a studio lot before the war, suddenly enlisted in the
cause of national cinema--and made small fortunes almost
overnight.

        The government of the Dual Monarchy continued to
exercise virtually no restraint on film-makers and distributors, except in areas of conventional Catholic morality.
There was no Austrian equivalent of the Russian Skobelev
Committee to mobilize the resources of the film industry on
behalf of the war effort.   Instead, the government successfully relied on the industry's commercial sense in maintaining a heavy output of patriotic war features that appealed to
the popular taste.   Alexander Korda's An Officer's Swordknot
(1915) was fairly typical of the genre: a Hussar officer dis-
graces himself and his regiment through gambling, re-enlists
as an ordinary soldier and distinguishes himself on the battlefield, winning back his rank and honor.   The film thus exalts
all the aristocratic qualities prized by the Hungarian half of
the Dual Monarchy.   According to the film, the Hungarian
armies were winning glorious victories on the road to the
inevitable defeat of the enemy.   The Hungarian nobility, which
was leading the fight, is characterized as endowed with inherent virtues, which can be clearly seen even when noble-
men are disguised as common people.   This theme remained
popular in Hungarian cinema for almost twenty years.

        The war-time boom collapsed in 1919, almost as sud-
denly as it had grown.   With the end of the war and the resulting depression, modern film-making equipment became
too costly to be purchased by Eastern European studios.
Austria-Hungary's former ally, Germany, and the United
States flooded the region with films that had been produced
during the war but which were new to the audience which had
lived under the blockade.   Croatia, formerly a major market
for Hungarian films, was closed off from Hungary by new
national frontiers.   A similar situation developed in relation
to the Viennese market for Czech-made films.   Transylvania
was annexed away from Hungary, whose film-makers lost not
only the extensive market for their work but also the use of
the Kolozsvar Studios.   The film-makers of Warsaw, however,
gained a new large market with the creation of a Polish

national state. It was a confusing year for the region in general; in film-making, 1919 can only be described as chaotic.

Intellectuals such as Alexander Korda in Hungary and Miroslav Urban in Czechoslovakia desperately tried to stem the second collapse of their national film industries through continued production and the organization of film-makers' unions. In Warsaw, film-making became dominated by the actors and producers of the legitimate theater. Although this domination had serious consequences for the later creativity of Polish cinema, the continued support of the film industry by the extremely successful Polish theater enabled film production to continue in Warsaw at a modest level while elsewhere in Eastern Europe it was becoming moribund.

Cinema under Bela Kun

In March, 1919, the feeble democratic government of Hungary fell under the control of a disciple of Lenin, Bela Kun. The new Communist dictatorship immediately seized the privately-owned means of communication, including the financially shaky Hungarian film industry. A National Film Council was created during the first two weeks of the new regime to encourage the production of films depicting stories from world and Hungarian literature. As Kun's government became aware that an independent film industry could not survive the pressure of foreign competition, it acted to nationalize film production. An official government production company, the Motion Picture Directorate, was created in May and placed under the direct supervision of Bela Pavlik, a member of the ruling Council of Peoples' Commissars and a close friend of the dictator. The nationalization was completed on April 12, 1919, four months before a similar action was begun in the Soviet Union.

As in the early days of Soviet film production, government involvement in the film industry was limited under Bela Pavlik primarily to supplying the financial and logistic support to "approved" film-makers. The Communists attempted to rely upon the uncertain political convictions of their leftist film-makers to provide acceptable ideological content. The few guidelines established by Pavlik called for the maintenance of a high "intellectual" level for the national film industry. As a result of this policy, most of the Hungarian film production during the summer of 1919 consisted of adaptations of classic literary works designed to raise the cultural

awareness of the average Hungarian. Budapest audiences
were subjected to a flood of hurriedly-produced versions of
such novels as War and Peace, The Brothers Karamazov
and the historical romances of Geza Gardonyi.

   Officially, the government-owned film industry consisted of four "official" scenarists, twelve "official" directors
and two hundred and fifty-three actors and technicians. Of
these, the burden of management fell upon the same men
who had been active during the war years, notably Korda,
the actor Bela Lugosi and the director Mihaly Kertesz. Although none of these prominent figures were Communists,
they attempted to respond favorably to the government's support of their industry by producing motion pictures in support of Pavlik's ideological objectives. A third director,
Bela Balogh, became a specialist in political comedy, despite his apparent lack of political convictions.

   Balogh's comedy depended on its story line for the
presentation of its political message. In The Doll, a typical
Balogh film, a young novice in a monastery suddenly loses
interest in religion when he inherits a large fortune. Anxious to keep him--and the inheritance--in the monastery, the
other monks manufacture an artificial girl to keep the young
man content. Fortunately, the novice's real friends substitute a live girl for the doll and the two leave the monastery
to live happily ever after. In effect, The Doll was little
more than the low comedy film common during the post-war
period, despite its slightly anti-religious overtones. While
this kind of material was probably ineffective as support for
anti-Church propaganda, it was far more popular than the
literary adaptations. It also succeeded in antagonizing the
conservative, Catholic elements of Hungary who came to
view the film industry as a Zionist plot against true Hungarian culture.

   The bloody "Red Terror" instituted by the Communists
and the failure of Bela Kun to defeat an invading Rumanian
army led to the sudden collapse of the regime on August 1,
1919. Budapest was occupied and sacked by the Rumanians
while Hungarian monarchists took revenge on suspected Communists, particularly Jewish intellectuals. Korda, Kertesz,
Lugosi and many other prominent film-makers immediately
fled into exile. A few other directors, notably Sandor Pallos,
Bela Geroffy and Bela Balogh, remained in Budapest. Only
Balogh escaped death or imprisonment at the hands of the
monarchists. Overnight, the extremely productive film colony
in Budapest vanished.

The approximately one hundred days' existence of the Motion Picture Directorate of Hungary resulted in the production of thirty-one feature films, all but one of which are lost today. This unprecedented rate of production was the least important legacy of the experiment. The vitality generated within the industry by government sponsorship was carried to Western Europe and the United States by the exiled Hungarian directors and actors. Alexander Korda became the most successful British producer. His younger brothers Vincent and Zoltan accompanied him to London where they gained reputations respectively as a set designer and director. Kertesz became the Hollywood director Michael Curtiz and Bela Lugosi returned to the legitimate theater where he eventually became typecast as Count Dracula.

Peoples' Commissar Bela Pavlik escaped the White Terror by fleeing to the Soviet Union. While it cannot be proven that his presence there directly influenced the Soviet film industry, it is interesting to note that the first nationalized film studios in Russia were organized within two weeks of Pavlik's arrival. The initial structure of the nationalized industry in Russia seems to have been patterned after the Hungarian Motion Picture Directorate, although the limited degree of ideological control essential to creativity under the Directorate was quickly replaced by stricter control in Russia. Thus, the two most important aspects of the Directorate period of Hungarian film-making--the intense creativity of individual directors and its bureaucratic administration--survived long after the fall of the Bela Kun regime.

Within Hungary, however, film-making was doomed. With most of its personnel in prison, in exile or executed and its studios in ruins (except, miraculously, the old Hunnia lot), the film industry could have been maintained only with heavy government subsidy. The new reactionary dictatorship of Admiral Miklos Horthy was not interested in rebuilding the "Jewish-dominated" industry. A further blow to Hungarian film-making was delivered in 1920, when the government authorized the re-establishment of the Projectograph film distribution monopoly. As before, Projectograph discouraged local production by favoring the presentation of imported films.

Bela Balogh and others attempted to maintain a national film industry in Hungary with antiquated equipment and decreasing supplies of capital. Balogh's best-known film, No Kissing, a satire about an inept dictator who outlaws

kissing, is a product of the post-Directorate period. Such
efforts further antagonized the Horthy regime. The few remaining Hungarian film-makers were unable to resist the
pressures of government censorship, foreign competition and
the Projectograph monopoly. In 1928, the last active film
studio in Budapest closed its gates and Hungarian film-making
ceased to exist.

Slow Rebirth in Czechoslovakia and Poland

In Czechoslovakia and Poland, recovery from the post-
war crash of their film studios' fortunes proceeded slowly
throughout the 1920's. The impact of the crash was far less
in Warsaw than in Prague, partly because of the intense nationalism of the newly-independent Polish state. From 1919
until 1923, veteran Polish directors such as Wiktor Bieganski
and Edward Puchalski worked with nothing except patriotic
spectacles. Bieganski's Pan Twardowski (1921) and Puchalski's Year 1863 (1922) glorified historic incidents in Polish
history. Literary works adapted for the film medium during
this period were chosen for their nationalist sentiments;
Puchalski's Tojemnica Medallion (1922), for example, was a
popular treatment of an extremely anti-Russian historical
novel.

A second factor which helped the Polish national film
industry to survive the post-war crash was the continued interest in the film medium among the owners and actors of
legitimate theaters. Theater owners considered a locally-
produced newsreel or "educational" film to be a valuable addition to the theater program, usually preceding the presentation of a longer stage piece. For this reason, the best of
the early Polish directors--Aleksander Ford and Leonard
Buczkowski--were attracted to documentary production. Stage
actors saw cinema as a second source of income and flocked
to the studios of Wiktor Bieganski. By 1922, Bieganski had
become famous for such speedily-directed features as Jealousy
and Abyss of Repentance (both 1923). There was little that
was distinctively Polish in his repetitive stories of women
who "give in to the baser passions" and repent, occasionally
too late. Nevertheless, Bieganski and the moonlighting legitimate stage actors maintained the financial stability of his
small studios at a time when other Polish directors were
leaving for Berlin and Hollywood.

During the late 1920's, a third major influence on the

future of Polish cinema appeared.   The Society of Devotees
of the Artistic Film (START), an organization of militant
young film-makers, was instrumental in establishing a distinctively Polish style of film-making.   Founded in 1920 by
Wanda Jacubowska, a student of fine arts at Warsaw University, the START expanded rapidly in membership and influence
after 1927.   By 1929, START included Aleksander Ford, at
21 already one of Poland's leading directors, and Jerzy
Toeplitz, Poland's foremost film critic and founder of the
Lodz School of Film-Making in 1945.   START advocated an
escape from the stylistic influence of the dramatic theater
and encouraged its members to experiment in uncompromising
realism.   Members of the society competed in directing the
most "honest" documentaries, occasionally tainted with socialist propaganda, such as Wild Fields (1932) and The Pulse
of Poland's Manchester (1929).   The resulting style of direction was similar to the "neo-realist" movement in post-war
Italian cinema.

Despite the activities of START, however, the less
controversial work of Bieganski and his imitators remained
more popular with Polish audiences than the radically realist
documentaries.   Gradually, the "young Turks" grew older
and many lost their radicalism in the face of financial mis-
fortune and the increasing censorship of film by the conservative regime of Marshal Jozef Pilsudski.   Although a few
of its members, including Ford, Jacubowska and Toeplitz,
remained true to the guiding principles of the society, START
itself was dissolved in 1935.

The Czech cinema was almost destroyed by the same
forces of foreign competition and domestic distribution monopoly which ended film production in Hungary.   Many Czech directors left the country in 1919, fearing the total collapse of
the national film-making industry.   In 1923, the directors of
the A-B Studio in Prague filed for bankruptcy, but an influx
of fresh capital saved the last Czech film studio before bankruptcy proceedings were completed.   During the three years
which followed, Czech film-making slowly struggled towards
financial security.   By 1926, there was a large enough market for Czech films to permit the establishment of a successful local competitor to A-B Studios, Kavalika Studios.   At
the same time, Czech cinema developed its own stylistic
characteristics.   Czech directors gained a reputation throughout Europe for their frank portrayal of human emotions in
everyday, intimate situations.   The development of this style
was aided by the traditional Czech humanistic philosophy and

by the extreme leniency of the democratic Czech government's censorship policies. Unfortunately, almost no works survive from this crucial period in the development of Czech cinema.

It is certain that one of the directors who led the early Czech movement for a humanistic cinema was Gustav Machaty. Machaty had emigrated to Hollywood in 1921, where he had been an assistant director to such German emigré film-makers as Erich von Stroheim. Returning to his homeland in 1925, he helped to organize the new Kavalika Company. Machaty's first feature as a director, The Kreutzer Sonata (1926), was based on the short story by Tolstoy. Set in a train compartment, the film analyzes the psychology of a passenger who has just murdered his wife and her lover. Using flash-backs and various camera speeds to set the mood, Machaty displayed great promise in his ability to depict complex motivation without the use of sound. For this reason, The Kreutzer Sonata can be said to have been years ahead of its time in its style.

Machaty's next film, Erotikon (1928), also centered on the theme of Man confronted with the evil within him. In narrating the fall from virtue of a railroad station-master's daughter, Machaty abandoned the Victorian moralizing of contemporary film-makers, including Bieganski of Poland and D. W. Griffith in the United States. The heroine of Erotikon ends badly; first seduced by a passing stranger and later one of the "harem" of a wealthy, decadent young man in Prague. As in the Kreutzer Sonata, Machaty experimented with stylistic details which were considered extremely avantgarde in 1928 but which are accepted as commonplace today; the seduction scene, for example, is seen almost entirely as a series of close-ups of the lovers' heads, eyes and mouths.

By 1929, the relatively conservative and nationalist government of Prime Minister Antonin Svehla was becoming concerned with the growth of nationalism among the Slovaks and Germans living in Czechoslovakia. Eventually, these forces of minority nationalism helped to destroy the first Czechoslovak Republic, but in 1929 the Czech government was unwilling to do more than propagandize on behalf of "Czechoslovak" nationalism. As part of this propaganda effort, the Czech government commissioned the production of a small number of patriotic feature films. This action was one of the few instances in Eastern Europe of a democratic regime directly subsidizing specific films.

The most popular of these patriotic features, <u>Colonel Svec</u>, featured the military strength of the new republic. The thin plot of an officer who sacrifices his life and honor for the regiment had to compete with an extensive display of uniformed troops and weapons. The historical spectacle, <u>St. Wenceslaus</u> (1929), a biography of the Czech patron saint, failed to capture the public's imagination and led to the end of the government subsidy of patriotic features by the summer of 1930.

Despite the loss of the subsidy, many of the Czech directors continued to make feature films glorifying the Czech national traditions. These latter patriotic works were generally biographies of Czech artists, writers and political leaders, as in <u>Karl Borovsky</u> (1930) and <u>Bedrich Smetana</u> (1931). Directed by the best talent of A-B Studios and Kavalika, the film biographies attempted to humanize the national heroes and make them familiar to the German and Slovak minorities. Instead, the patriotic films tended to increase the nationalism of the Czech half of the population while doing little to endear the regime to the national minorities.

The failure of Czech cinema to promote a "Czechoslovak nationalism" went almost unnoticed by contemporary critics. They were far more concerned with the numerous successes, both artistic and financial, of the industry. By 1930, the films of Machaty and his colleague, Svatopluk Inneman, were being successfully exported to Germany, France and the United States. There was no question that the Czech film industry had the greatest vitality of the national cinemas of Eastern Europe.

The Zenith of Nationalist Cinema, 1930-1940

Two events occurred in 1929 which led to the most productive period of motion picture production in Eastern European history. The first was the announcement by a Czech inventor, Josef Slechta, that he had perfected a device which recorded sound directly onto motion picture film. This was not the first "sound camera" to be invented nor was it the last. Walt Disney's <u>Steamboat Willie</u> had employed a similar technique in the previous year. Nevertheless, invention of a sound camera by a Czech citizen meant that Eastern European studios would not be dependent on expensive sound equipment from Germany or the United States. Eastern European audiences soon flocked to the theaters to

hear their own local film stars talk and sing in their national
languages. At the same time, imported films with French,
German or English dialogue became unprofitable except in the
cities and a few rural areas with heavy German populations.

The other crucial event was "Black Tuesday," October 29, when the stock market "crashed" in New York and
initiated a world-wide depression. Governments quickly became conscious of the meaning of "balance of payments" and
"economic self-sufficiency." In an effort to save their crum-
bling currencies, the governments of Eastern Europe abandoned their free trade policies and resorted to high tariffs
and import quotas. In terms of world trade, these protec-
tive actions were a mistake, but for local industries the high
tariff walls were a blessing. Among the national enterprises
aided by the new government economic policies were the local film industries.

Hungary, still under the dictatorship of Admiral
Horthy, was one of the first nations to support its national
cinema actively during the Great Depression. Although unwilling to destroy the Projectograph film distribution monopoly, the Horthy government was painfully aware that Projectograph's policy of favoring imported features was hurting the
Hungarian balance of payments. In late 1930, the government
decided to revive the Hungarian film-making industry which
it had helped to destroy only two years before. The Hunnia
Studios in Budapest became the government-owned State Film
Studio, available for the use of any Hungarian producer who
wished to participate in the government program. New taxes
and import duties were charged on films imported by Projectograph. When this action failed to achieve the result of forcing the distribution monopoly to change its policies, the
Horthy government attempted to impose a law declaring that,
for every twenty foreign films distributed in Hungary, at
least one Hungarian-produced film must be distributed. Projectograph and its suppliers in Hollywood threatened to re-
taliate by boycotting Hungarian distribution entirely. The
Horthy government was cowed into revoking the ratio law and
substituting a fine on movie theaters which failed to present
at least one Hungarian film out of every twenty features
shown. The receipts from the fines became a "Film Industry
Fund" used to subsidize Hungarian producers.

Despite government cooperation, the State Film Studio
was not used very heavily during the first three years of its
existence. From 1930 until 1933, production averaged only

ten feature films a year.   After 1933, however, the extensive use of sound increased the Hungarian audiences' desire
for locally-produced films, particularly musicals.

The musical film dominated Hungarian cinema throughout the remainder of the 1930's and the early 1940's.   This
was due, in part, to the preferences of the Hungarian government.   As soon as the "Film Industry Fund" reached major
proportions, the Horthy regime created a National Film Committee to censor the screenplays of any producer who wished
to receive a part of the subsidy or use the State Film Studios.
The Film Committee consisted of aging aristocrats and military officers who had little knowledge of motion pictures.
Like those of Horthy himself, the political beliefs of the
Committee consisted primarily of nostalgia for the by-gone
days of the Hapsburg Empire and the unchallenged rule of
the Magyar landowners over their estates and their nation.
Thus, any producer who catered to their tastes with nostalgic
romantic films set in the previous century and filled with the
splendid Hungarian ballads was certain to gain the respect
and approval of the Film Committee--and a large subsidy.

The most successful of the Hungarian musical films
of the 1930's was Rakosci March, directed in 1934 by Istvan
Szekely.   Admiral Horthy, then 66 years old and at the
height of his power and influence, publicly declared Rakosci
March to be his favorite film.   In New York City, the Times
reported that large crowds of Hungarians and Hungarian-
Americans stood in lines for hours at the little Tobis theater
in Yorktown to see the film when it first opened there in
1935.

Despite the attention that the Rakosci March drew to
itself, as a work of art it is unimpressive.   Set in and
around Budapest at the turn of the century, the thin plot concerns the courting of a supposedly wealthy girl by a poor
but aristocratic cavalry officer.   The film's only dramatic
scene occurs when the girl's unjustly indignant brother chal-
lenges the officer to a duel and the hero must decide between
risking his honor or the life of the brother of the girl he
loves.   In true aristocratic fashion, he decides to save his
honor and accepts the challenge.   Happily, however, it is
discovered that the girl is not wealthy and that the brother
has no cause to take offense.   Thus, as in so many other
Hungarian films of the period, Rakosci March "proves" that
it was possible to live in the twentieth century by the Medieval code of honor of the Hungarian upper classes and still

Fig. 2. Istvan Szekely directing the lead in <u>Rakosci March</u> (Source: Private collection of Istvan Szekely)

live happily ever after. This was the philosophy of the members of the National Film Committee as reflected in the films
which they censored and subsidized.

The Hungarians did not love Rakosci March either for
its weak plot or its bizarre morality. It was perfectly possible for a leftist Hungarian intellectual in exile in New York
to consider the plot of the film absurd and its philosophy re-
pellent, yet nevertheless go to see the film five or six times
for its nostalgic music and its brilliantly photographed scenes
of Budapest and the surrounding countryside. A critic from
Communist Hungary, in a recent discussion of Rakosci March,
argued strongly against the film's political and social content
but ended his presentation with: "All that I have said is true
but ... Oh! those Hungarian songs!"

Rakosci March was followed by literally dozens of
similar films, characterized by turn-of-the-century settings,
weak plots and a great number of musical interludes.
Szekely's Purple Acacia (1936) was an attempt to better the
success of the Rakosci March by featuring the most popular
Hungarian actress, singer Irene Agai, and the most popular
Hungarian comedian, Gyula Kabos. As usual, the film was
set in Budapest prior to World War I and the story is a typical romantic triangle between the poor and innocent heroine
(Agai), a wealthy young nobleman who meets her in the park
and a vain young society woman who wants to marry him for
position. The sentimentality of Purple Acacia is still appreciated in modern Hungary; in 1972, the Hungarian government invited Szekely to return to Budapest for the first time
in 35 years to direct a grandiose color remake of the film.

There were few serious dramas among the Hungarian
films of the 1930's; they were nearly never as popular as
musicals. When a drama was produced, the Film Committee preferred it to have a pre-1918 setting, to underscore
patriotic virtues and aristocratic morality and to have a happy
ending. In effect, the Committee wanted modern versions of
An Officer's Swordknot.

Istvan Szekely's Only One Night (1935) was typical of
the patriotic drama desired by the Film Committee. Set on
the Russian front during the First World War, it begins with
a well-directed battle scene. The story develops when a
young Hungarian officer finds the wife of a Russian general
abandoned on the battlefield and refuses to help her return
to the Russian lines because he is in the midst of an attack.

Fig. 3. Istvan Szekely directing Irene Agai (Source: Private collection of Istvan Szekely)

Shortly afterwards, the Hungarian is captured and sentenced to death by the unscrupulous Russians as a spy, despite the fact that he was found on the battlefield in uniform and had surrendered honorably. Happily, he is rescued by the wife of the Russian commander, who is none other than the woman he discovered behind the Hungarian lines at the beginning of the film. Despite his unchivalric action, she has fallen in love with him and she now helps him return to his regiment while she abandons her brutal husband. Only One Night was not among the most popular Hungarian films, although critics admitted that the background music was pleasant.

The only Hungarian films which depicted contemporary Hungary during the 1930's were comedies, popular with both the urban audiences and the National Film Committee. The most successful and best-known of the comedies produced during this period was Dream Car, directed in 1934 by Bela Gaal. This was nothing more than a modern version of the Cinderella story, with a typist falling in love with the general manager of her company who has disguised himself as a chauffeur. When they visit a resort together, the girl is insulted by a nouveau riche member of the bourgeoisie--a frequent villain in Hungarian films of this period--but is defended by her lover, who is now revealed as man of honor and good family.

Istvan Nemeskurty, the prominent Hungarian film historian, claims that from 1934 through 1938, no less than seventy-five films were produced by Hungarian studios after the pattern of Dream Car. They were characterized by catchy title songs, inconsequential romantic plots and consistent reiteration of the idea that the aristocracy embodied all the best in Hungarian national character while the nouveau riche embodied decadence. By 1936, the ideological control of the National Film Committee became more positive; suggestions were made by the committee members on what to include in motion pictures in addition to what had to be censored. Directors were encouraged to include brief scenes of military maneuvers or modern industrial plants in the midst of their comic plots in order to remind the audience of the Horthy regime's progress in modernizing the country.

One strange result of the Film Committee's new policy was a film entitled Half-Rate Honeymoon (1936). Two years before, Hungary had signed a treaty of military and commercial cooperation with Fascist Italy, including a clause which implied that tourism between the two nations would be encouraged. In 1936, Italy offered a "package honeymoon tour" to foreign newlyweds, with hotels and transportation at half-rates. Istvan Szekely was encouraged to direct a romantic comedy that would increase interest in the tour among Hungarians. The resulting film centered on the travels of two Hungarian couples, one newlywed and the other pretending, who take advantage of the Italian government's generous offer. The center of attraction of Half-Rate Honeymoon was neither the thin plot nor the acting but the extremely well-photographed views of Italian hotels, cities, ocean liners and countryside.

Szekely's next comedy, An Affair of Honor (1937), was the most politically significant film to be made in Hungary between the wars. Critics outside of Hungary saw nothing controversial in the simple story of a kind, but thoughtless youth who atones for forcing an old office manager at his uncle's factory into quitting his job by marrying his victim's pretty daughter. Within Hungary, however, An Affair of Honor provoked violent reactions. Supporters of the Horthy regime were furious to see the old office manager, brilliantly played by Gyula Kabos, transformed into a hero by sacrificing his job rather than dueling with the arrogant young aristocrat. The film was considered a satirical critique of the upper classes' code of honor and this may, in fact, have been the intention of both Szekely and Kabos. Angry young students rioted in Budapest against the film, while the government leaders hinted darkly that Szekely and Kabos were more Zionist than Hungarian.

In 1938, the policies of Hungarian prime minister Kalman Daranyi towards Hungarian Jews and in foreign affairs became visibly more fascistic. Although Daranyi was soon replaced by a more moderate lieutenant of Admiral Horthy, it was clear that Hungary would remain allied to Nazi Germany and Fascist Italy. Another massive wave of emigration among the Hungarian film-makers resulted. Szekely became "Steve Sekely" in Hollywood, a prolific director, first in film and later in television. Kabos also went into exile in the United States, but he failed to succeed in his new career as a vaudeville performer. Other Hungarian film-makers left to work for Korda in England or for Curtiz in the United States.

This second wave of emigration did not result in the destruction of Hungarian film-making as an industry. Instead, opportunistic producers and second-rate directors willing to

accept the Film Committee's increasingly tight ideological
control replaced the departing talent.   From 1939 until 1944,
Hungarian cinema was characterized by anti-semitic propaganda and by old-fashioned melodramas.   Typical of the wartime dramas, <u>Light and Shadow</u> (1941) depicted the weak-
willed aristocrat who deserts his saintly wife for a lower-
class vamp.   The sinful woman eventually scorns the stray-
ing husband after having thoroughly corrupted him, while the
wife forgets her sorrows by turning their villa into an asylum
for working-class orphans.   It was clear that the Film Committee's propaganda on behalf of aristocratic morality was
increased in intensity during the war years.   On the other
hand, the Committee's flamboyant anti-semitism and general
incompetence resulted in a steady decline of quality and
creativity during the 1940's.

Czech and Polish Cinema during the 1930's

Czech cinema before the German occupation continued
to display the humanistic philosophy of Czech intellectuals.
Most of the directors who had been active during the silent
era in the Prague film colony continued to work during the
1930's.   Their experience in working without sound led many
Czech directors to continue to emphasize lighting, editing
and cinematography to depict moods and emotions, rather
than depend solely on dialogue.   Svatoplok Inneman's <u>The
Third Troop</u> (1931), for example, has no leading actors and
almost no dialogue.   Instead, Inneman used scenes of Czech
soldiers drilling together, working and lounging around the
barracks, to illustrate the comradeship within the republic's
armed forces.   As a patriotic film, it was far more effective than it could have been had the director resorted to nationalistic narration or ringing speeches of Czech pride.

Similarly, Gustav Machaty's later feature films depended on his expertise in the direction of camerawork rather
than on his ability to direct actors for his work's emotional
impact.   In 1934, Machaty achieved world-wide notoriety for
<u>Ecstasy</u>, a film starring the popular Hedy Kiesler.   The film
was essentially the story of a romantic triangle involving the
heroine, her much older husband and her lover.   The Czech
censors realized that Machaty's intentions in the direction of
<u>Ecstasy</u> were not pornographic and approved the film's re-
lease shortly after its completion.   Outside liberal Czechoslovakia, however, the extremely brief glimpse of Miss
Kiesler in the nude and the very concept that a sympathetic

Fig. 4. Hedy Kiesler (Lamarr) in Machaty's Ecstasy.
Courtesy, Museum of Modern Art.

character should be portrayed as enjoying an illicit rendez-
vous with a lover raised a storm of controversy. In the
United States, presentation of the film was delayed until
1940. Even after the six-year delay, American censors insisted that 25 feet of Ecstasy be edited, and an explanation
was added to the effect that the young lovers were secretly
married before their romantic tryst in a deserted cabin.
Similar "improvements" were made to the film as presented
in other countries. Only in Italy, where the film won a
major prize, was Ecstasy shown in the original, uncut version.

Ecstasy marked a highpoint both in the career of
Gustav Machaty and in the history of Czech cinema. Shortly
after completing the film, Machaty returned to Hollywood
where he quickly became lost in the bustling film colony of
the 1930's. After the Second World War, he emigrated to
Germany, where he regained some of his former reputation
as a screenplay writer before his death in 1963. His star,
Hedy Kiesler, was far more fortunate. She followed Machaty
to Hollywood a few years later and began a highly successful
career as the American actress Hedy Lamarr.

The departure of Machaty marked the beginning of a
decline in the creativity of the Prague film colony. The
frankness and lyricism of Ecstasy spawned a series of imitations, of which the most successful was Ecstasy of Young
Love, directed in 1935 by J. Bodensky. Bodensky attempted
to capture Machaty's naturalistic style of direction by using
untrained actors and actresses in the leading roles and by
making the greatest possible use of studies of flowers and
landscape throughout the film. Unfortunately, Bodensky and
Machaty's other imitators relied heavily on dialogue and
avoided plots which might be considered controversial abroad.
Ecstasy of Young Love, for example, lacks the dramatic conflict of Ecstasy's romantic triangle. In place of the opposition of society to the lovers, Bodensky substitutes a stern
father who disapproves of his wealthy son being in love with
a poor girl. Thus, the possible social comment of the film
is lost in the saccharine story.

A probable cause for this reduction of creativity in
Czech cinema during the 1930's was the realization that the
standards of the export market for films were very different
from those accepted by liberal Czech audiences. Directors
abandoned frankness to avoid the censure of foreign critics;
they sacrificed the honest examination of human relationships

inherent in the Czech humanist tradition to cater to foreign sentimentality.

A second force which contributed to the decline of Czech cinema as an intellectual art form was Slovak nationalism. Prior to 1919, Slovakia had been a peasant region under the authoritarian control of Hungary. There was little opportunity for the development of Slovak culture. With the creation of the Czechoslovak republic, this situation was changed. Slovak "patriots" began to demand cultural and political autonomy as a reaction to the domination of the republic by the more numerous Czechs. By 1935, these demands had developed into a militant nationalism among many Slovak intellectuals.

In film, this nationalism was expressed in a series of productions glorifying the Slovak historical tradition. Although Slovakia did not produce a qualified director until 1945, Slovaks were active in screenwriting, acting and other aspects of production of their own historical spectacles throughout the 1930's. By far, the most successful of these was Janosik (1936), directed by the veteran Czech director Martin Frič. Janosik was a highly fictionalized biography of an 18th-century Slovak bandit. The superb technical quality of the work made the film popular in both the Czech and Slovak regions and abroad. The Czech Frič has continued to specialize in producing similar works until the present day, but his Janosik was a trend-setting film in its decade.

Two years later, the Munich agreements resulted in the de facto destruction of Czechoslovakia, a situation made more permanent by Nazi occupation in March, 1939. Film production was greatly diminished under the Nazis, although Frič and a handful of other directors found work catering to the needs of the new "independent" Slovak state. This period in Czech film history, however, belongs more properly to the study of the motion picture industry of the Third Reich.

Polish cinema during the 1930's did not change greatly. An economic slump during the early years of the decade caused a corresponding decline in film production. Most of the output of the Warsaw studios were either insipid literary adaptations, usually of Polish novels and plays, or low-budget historical spectacles. The year 1937 marked the foundation of the Co-operative of Screenplay Authors, composed primarily of leftist writers, but the efforts of the organization remained clearly within the extensive literary tradition of Poland.

The major development of the decade was the institution of increasingly severe political censorship by the ruling National Unity Front, a parliament bloc controlled by the extremely nationalistic Polish military. The purpose of the censorship was to discourage the socialist propaganda inserted in the works of many Polish directors, particularly Alexander Ford. This was clearly seen in the reaction to Ford's feature Street (1932) and his documentary The Children Must Laugh (1936). The earlier film, a painfully realistic story of a boy from the Warsaw slums who must work selling newspapers to support an injured mother, resulted in much controversy within Poland. The socialists praised the film for its honest view of the exploitation of child labor; the nationalists attacked it for depicting the poverty of the Warsaw slums. Despite the polemics of either side, the film was freely shown, both in Poland and abroad.

The Children Must Laugh, a semi-documentary made only four years later, was banned within Poland. In this case, the subject of the work--a children's tuberculosis sanitarium financed by Jewish labor unions--was not controversial. Instead, the authorities objected to a single scene in which the 185 inmates of the institution volunteer to give bed space to the children of striking Polish workers.

A second development of Polish cinema in the 1930's was the reappearance of extremely militaristic, patriotic spectacles, similar in many respects to those which characterized Hungarian cinema during the same period. Such films were encouraged by the military leaders of the Polish government as a counterbalance to the work of the socialist film-makers. Hearts Aflame (1937), directed by Romuald Gantkowski, was reminiscent of Edward Puchalski's earlier works. Frequent scenes of barracks life, maneuvers, and military balls were occasionally interrupted by a romance between a young officer and the daughter of a nobleman. Red Rose (1938), directed by Josef Lejtes, created a vogue for anti-Russian stories of the Polish revolutions against the Tsar. Keyed to the anti-Soviet propaganda line of the Polish government, Red Rose featured scenes of Russians brutally questioning innocent Poles while the Warsaw revolutionaries are spurred to attack by Chopin's Revolutionary Etude.

As the Second World War approached, nationalism within Poland reached new heights. On the eve of hostilities, the leftist elements of the Polish film industry began to respond to the mushrooming demand for patriotic features.

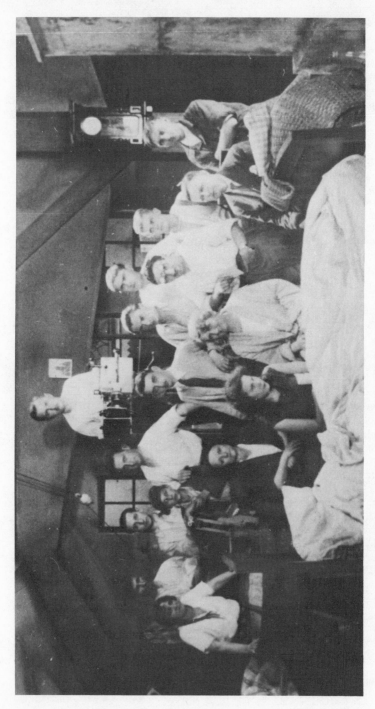

Fig. 5. Alexander Ford (center, with necktie) directing Street (Source: Film Polski)

Even Wanda Jacubowska, the former leader of the radical
START group, contributed by directing an adaptation of the
nationalist novel, On the Nieman (1939).

The war and the Nazi conquest completely destroyed
the Polish film industry. The studios in Warsaw and Cracow
were levelled during the initial fighting and most of the Polish
film-makers who remained in Poland during the occupation
were placed in concentration camps. A handful, led by the
now flagrantly Communist Alexander Ford, escaped to the
Soviet Union where they organized the Polish Army Film
Command in 1943. This unit accompanied the Red Army on
its liberation of Poland, producing a comprehensive film record of the war, the Nazi occupation and the Nazi genocide
camps. Majdanek (1944), a documentary by Ford filmed
during the first liberation of a "death camp," was reportedly
used as evidence during the Nuremberg trials.

Balkan Experiments in Film

        Of the five Balkan states--Yugoslavia (or the Kingdom
of the Serbs, Croats and Slovenes), Bulgaria, Rumania,
Greece and Albania--only Yugoslavia had any film production
prior to 1930. Croatia Film, founded in 1919, was basically
a part of the legacy of the Austro-Hungarian Empire's widespread film industry. It collapsed financially in 1920 after
producing only one feature. Two years later, Jugoslavija
Film moved into the abandoned studios of Croatia Film in
Zagreb. This second attempt was more successful, primarily
due to the patronage of the Croatian Peasant Party, the major political power among the Croats. Stepan Radić, the
flamboyant leader of the party, subsidized the struggling
film company which, in turn, provided him with political
propaganda films in support of his party's program. This
relationship was the only example in Eastern Europe of an
opposition party controlling the national film industry.
Through Radić's support, Jugoslavija Film earned enough
profits to open a School of Cinematography under the management of the company's leading director, Jovan Halla.

        In Belgrade, the government of Serbia looked with dis-
may at the Croatian monopoly of the Yugoslav film industry
and attempted to create a Serbian industry to counter the cultural and political influence of Jugoslavija Film. In 1924,
the government of the Serb nationalist Nicolas Pasić undertook the subsidy of the Filmophile Club. This was a small

group of Serbian intellectuals who discussed foreign films and
occasionally wrote articles in the local press calling for the
establishment of a film industry based in Belgrade. Pasić
quickly discovered that the subsidy was wasted. The Filmophile Club squandered the government funds on a series of
amateurish productions. Their only feature-length film, The
Brigands of Topeider (1925), was a poorly-executed satire
on the cherished tradition of 18th-century nationalist bandits
robbing from the Turkish oppressors and distributing the
wealth among the Serbian peasants. This was precisely the
kind of anti-nationalist film which Prime Minister Pasić did
not want. When it was released to the public, Pasić immediately withdrew government support from the dilettante film-
makers.

In 1926, a group of Slovene intellectuals founded Sava
Film in the Slovene capital of Ljubljana. A non-profit organization, Sava Film's sole purpose was to record the rap-
idly-disappearing dances, costumes and other aspects of folk
culture among the Slovenian peasantry.

During the 1930's, independent producers appeared in
Belgrade, using makeshift studios and antiquated silent film
equipment. Their efforts were encouraged by the Yugoslav
government, which imposed a quota of 100 meters of Yugo-
slavian-produced film for every 1,000 meters of foreign film
distributed in Yugoslavia. This law, enacted for the same
reasons of foreign exchange which led to similar legislation
in Hungary, had to be revoked in 1933. Yugoslav producers
could not supply features in sufficient quantity to conform to
the quota.

The major development of the 1930's in Yugoslav cinema was the appearance of animated cartoons in Zagreb.
The first, and most successful, of the pre-war animators
were the Maar brothers, German Jewish animators who fled
Nazi persecution. In 1933, they opened a studio for the
production of commercial advertising cartoons which were
shown in addition to the feature films in Croat theaters.
The Maar brothers laid the foundation for the Zagreb "school"
of animation which gained international prestige during the
1950's.

Under German and Italian occupation during the Second
World War, film production ended in Zagreb and Ljubljana.
In Belgrade, however, feature film production continued spo-
radically, beginning with the first Serbian "talkie" in 1942.

In Montenegro, leftist film-makers joined Tito's partisans to make a film record of their underground activities.

Bulgarian cinema during the 1930's was a personal crusade of one eccentric, Vassil Gendev. Faced with complete government indifference and public ridicule, Gendev pawned his wristwatch and his wife's jewelry to finance a series of entirely unprofitable silent films. Gendev died during the Second World War, but he is revered among Bulgarian film-makers as a pioneer of their industry and his primitive, poorly-photographed works are almost considered national treasures. However the world may judge his talent, it cannot be denied that international cinema has not produced many producers with Gendev's energy and enthusiasm.

The Greek cinema was begun in the mid-1930's with such works as Dr. Epameimodas (1936), an inconsequential romantic comedy financed by the Bedda brothers of Alexandria, Egypt, and directed by the Egyptian T. Bezrahi. During the late 1940's, the domestic Greek film industry, bankrupted by the war, fell under the artistic and financial domination of English directors and producers. This cultural influence has lessened only in recent years. For this reason, a detailed analysis of Greek cinema is not particularly pertinent in a history of Eastern European film.

Conclusions

    In summary, cinema in Eastern Europe throughout the interwar period underwent two phases of political development. In the first phase, approximately from 1919 until 1931, the social and political implications of film were dominated by the beliefs of individual film-makers. This was reflected by the mildly socialist leanings of Hungarian directors during the 100 days of the Motion Picture Directorate, by the nationalism of Bieganski and the Marxism of Ford, and by the intellectual humanism of liberal Czech directors. Government intervention in the content of cinema was limited, despite the rise and fall of democracies and dictators.

    During the second phase, from 1931 until the outbreak of the Second World War, governments took a much more serious view of the content of films shown to their citizens. Economic depression and political tension created increased nationalism, even in democratic Czechoslovakia. This was reflected in government subsidy of national film industries

Fig. 6. Vassil Gendev, pioneering Bulgarian film-maker
(Source: Bulgarofilm)

in Hungary and Yugoslavia, in patriotic spectacles in Slovakia,
Hungary and Poland, and in extensive censorship throughout
the region.

The Second World War all but eliminated film production beyond the Danube. The end of the war found the studios
destroyed, the production companies bankrupt, the film-makers
themselves in exile or dead. A nucleus of a post-war film
industry existed for Poland in the Communist-dominated Polish Army Film Command. Elsewhere, it was clear that
cinema would have to be completely recreated. In such
countries as Hungary and Czechoslovakia, forty years of
film-making experience was lost.

CHAPTER 4

THE STALINIST CINEMA, 1929-1946

On an unknown date in the summer of 1934, an audience composed of high Communist Party officials gathered shortly after midnight in the private film theater of the Kremlin. Included among the members of the select group were Josef V. Stalin; Andrei A. Zhdanov, the Central Committee's recently-appointed "expert" on cultural affairs; and Boris Z. Shumyatsky, manager of the Soviet film industry. These midnight film programs were not unusual. Stalin had already become a chronic insomniac and he often spent the early morning hours viewing Soviet films before their public premieres. This activity not only helped to pass the sleepless hours; it also permitted the dictator to give his final approval to the ideological content of new Soviet releases.

On the night in question, the film which occupied the attention of the Kremlin audience was Chapayev, a biography of a Red Army leader assassinated by the Whites during the Russian civil war. The directors were two young men named Vasiliev whose talent had been questioned by their colleagues at the Leningrad studios. The Party had already expressed its interest in the film by permitting the directors to use the best of the U.S.S.R.'s small supply of sound equipment and modern cameras. Now the success or failure of their work depended on the reaction of the ultimate critics in the Kremlin.

When the showing was over, Stalin gravely announced that Chapayev was "by far, the best film ever made in the Soviet Union." Shumyatsky was ordered to give the motion picture the greatest possible distribution and to arrange for prizes and medals for everyone involved in its production. Zhdanov was asked to arrange an extremely favorable press response when Chapayev was released to the public. By these few words, the success of the film and of the young directors, Georgi N. and Sergei D. Vasiliev, was assured.

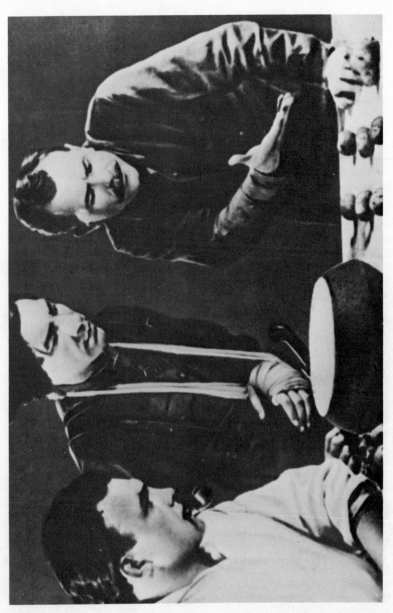

Fig. 7. <u>Chapayev</u>: teaching tactics with potatoes. (Source: Iskusstvo)

The leading actor in <u>Chapayev</u>, Boris Babotchkin, also received the benefits of Stalin's patronage ... for a while. In Babotchkin's later films, his mediocre talent was obvious, despite the lavish praises of Russian critics for Stalin's favorite. When no further encouragement came out of the Kremlin, the praise stopped and Babotchkin passed into the historical limbo reserved for second-rate Soviet actors.

The personalities and political beliefs of the three ultimate critics present that night in 1934 dominated all phases of Soviet cinema for a quarter of a century. Shumyatsky's management of the industry shaped the administrative bureaucracy within which Soviet film-makers had to work through 1954, despite the dismissal of Shumyatsky as an incompetent in 1938. Stalin's personal taste determined, in general, the kind of films which Soviet audiences could see during his lifetime. Zhdanov's policy statements on the doctrine of socialist realism provided Soviet cinema with guiding artistic and ideological principles. As a result, Soviet film-makers lost almost all control over the content of their work. In their place came the intellectual and ideological rule of Party theorists and bureaucrats.

The Proletarian Avant-garde: Proto-Socialist Realism

The Communist Party Central Committee's decision to impose a specific artistic movement on all creative workers in the Soviet Union developed slowly. A new "socialist" art had been advocated by some Bolsheviks as early as 1908. Leon Trotsky, in <u>Literature and Revolution</u>, called for a world literature that would be infused with revolutionary spirit and would reflect the class struggle. Immediately after the revolution, gangs of students often rode through the streets of Russian university towns, shouting out the lyrics of new, Red-sympathizing poets and declaring that pre-revolutionary art should be hidden in museums.

Throughout the 1920's, creative workers formed into assorted "schools" of proletarian art, each group insisting that they were the only true progressives and that competing groups were still bourgeois. The Party did not intervene in these controversies except to remind artists of Lenin's vague 1905 declaration that progressive art after the revolution must reflect "party spirit." During most of the 1920's, "reflecting party spirit" implied only that counter-revolutionary statements would not be tolerated. The resulting lack of

Party guidance fostered competition and resulted in a vast
amount of experimentation in all of the arts, including film.
The Pudovkin-Eisenstein debate over editing was merely part
of the clash of artistic ideas characteristic of the period.

Stalin disapproved of the chaotic situation in Soviet
arts. In his personal philosophy of Marxism-Leninism, as
expressed in numerous articles and speeches, socialist society must be viewed as a gigantic machine. The machine
ran well only if all its parts were coordinated and directed
towards the goals set by the Communist Party. Clearly, in
1928, the intellectual life of the Soviet Union was disorganized
and lacked coordination with the other elements of Soviet society. For Stalin, the only remedy was to impose organization and artistic guidelines on Soviet intellectuals, concentrating on authors and scenario writers.

The strong emphasis on controlling the writing staff
of the film industry can partly be explained by the relative
ease of censoring scenarios, as discussed in Chapter 1, and
partly by the background of the Communist Party leaders.
Most of the old Bolsheviks has been authors of written propaganda at some point in their revolutionary careers. Like
Stalin--the first editor of the newspaper Pravda--they under-
stood the propaganda value of words. They could not understand that the impact of motion pictures on an audience is
also dependent on images, moods, lighting and other variables
under the control of the director. The director of the film
was seen by them primarily as a glorified stage manager,
able to use his technical skill to bring the writer's concepts
into visual form. As late as 1971, conservative Communists
were still warning against "the cult of the director," the
Western concept that the director is higher in the film-making
hierarchy than the author of the scenario. With these prejudices, it is not surprising that artistic guidance of the film
industry by the Party centered on the contributions of the
scenario writer throughout the Stalinist era.

The first guidelines imposed were the strict censorship restraints formulated by the Main Administration on Affairs in Art and Literature during the winter of 1928-29.
This censorship consisted of many specific prohibitions.
Screenplays were forbidden from containing "slander"--any
negative comment--against the Communist Party, Komsomol,
Party members and any other "progressive" aspect of life in
the Soviet Union. Beginning with Eisenstein's Ten Days that
Shook the World (1927), all mention and film footage of

Trotsky and other discredited Party leaders were edited from
existing films.   Reference to these "traitors" in later films
was strictly regulated.   Finally, the heroes of all Soviet
screenplays had to be positive characters; no rogues, aristocrats or members of the bourgeoisie could be depicted as
sympathetic personalities and no anti-heroes could be featured.
This eliminated any possibility of filming several Russian
classics, including Gogol's The Inspector General and Dead
Souls.

        After being instructed by the Communist Party on
what they could not write, Soviet scenario authors continued
to dispute what they should write.   The most vocal "school"
of this time was a group of young, inexperienced film-makers
--mostly members of Komsomol--allied with a radical literary movement known as "the Proletarian Avant-garde."   In
general, they condemned the staff and students of the Moscow
State Film Institute for being over-concerned with art and
not concerned enough with political orthodoxy.   The Avant-
garde group boasted that the Komsomol youth were the ideological and cultural vanguard of the Soviet Union and that
they, as film-makers, were the only true representatives of
Lenin's views on film.

        Although the higher Party officials within the film in-
dustry were distressed by the disrespect of the Avant-garde
group for older Party members, they were willing to supply
them with money and equipment.   Only a handful of the
Avant-garde were Communist Party members, but their
stated ideological views, their reverence for Lenin and their
membership in Komsomol attested to their political orthodoxy.
In this respect, the Communist Party leadership believed
they were more reliable than the Moscow-trained directors.
Accordingly, in early 1929, Sergei Iosifovich Yutkevich, a
25-year-old set designer associated with the Avant-garde
group, was given permission to direct Black Sail.   Yutkevich's film was technically poor, due to his inexperience,
but the theme of Komsomol members demonstrating the benefits of a fishing cooperative to a village of suspicious fisher-
men fitted in perfectly with the propaganda needs of the
First Five-Year Economic Plan.   The Soviet leaders were
pleased with Black Sail and it seemed that the Proletarian
Avant-garde might triumph as the leading movement in Russian film.

        The following year, a 22-year-old actor, Alexander G.
Zarkhi (not to be confused with Natan Zarkhi, a scenario

writer closely associated with Pudovkin), and a 24-year-old
writer, Iosif Yefimovich Kheifits, received permission to direct jointly the first feature to be made solely by members
of the Proletarian Avant-garde group. The film, Facing the
Wind, attempted to document the role which Komsomol played
in eliminating bourgeois aspects of Russian society. Red
youth were shown running amok in an inn--smashing bottles,
breaking kegs, haranguing the innkeeper--as part of their
anti-alcoholism campaign. Unfortunately for Zarkhi and
Kheifits, Facing the Wind was completed at a time when the
Communist Party leadership was attempting to restrain the
violence of Komsomol. The two directors were accused of
misrepresenting Komsomol activities, despite the accuracy
of their characterization of the radicals within the youth organization. Fortunately for their later careers, their first
film was never completely banned and they were permitted
to remain together as a team. Nevertheless, the distribution
of Facing the Wind was severely limited by the film industry
managers and the film's failure to reflect the changed Party
attitude towards Komsomol radicalism ruined the reputation
of the Proletarian Avant-garde as a movement.

        The year 1930 was an equally unlucky one for Alek-
sandr P. Dovzhenko, the leading director at the Ukrainian
State Film Studios in Kiev. Born in 1896 in a Ukrainian
village, Dovzhenko had been a painter and a Soviet diplomat
before drifting into the film industry during the mid-1920's.
By the end of the decade, he had four successful films to
his credit (e.g., Zvenigora, released in 1928, and Arsenal,
released in 1929) and enjoyed a reputation for political reliability.

        Primarily because he was the only major director to
come from a peasant background, the Party chose Dovzhenko
in 1929 to film a definitive motion picture on agricultural
collectivization. The resulting film is Dovzhenko's best-
known work, Earth. Critics outside the U.S.S.R. immediately recognized Earth as a brillantly poetic work, filled
with images of fertility and growth and affectionate scenes
of peasants working their fields. The Soviet leadership,
however, disapproved. The members of the Party apparatus
did not understand how Dovzhenko's imagery helped the collectivization propaganda campaign. Instead, they found elements in Earth which were seemingly counter-revolutionary.
For example, the classic symbol of farm mechanization--a
tractor--was shown to be ugly, inefficient and subject to frequent breakdowns. The peasants are depicted as holding it

in complete contempt. This was definitely not the attitude towards tractors and rural progress desired by the Party in 1930. Earth, like Facing the Wind, contained propaganda in direct opposition to the current needs of the Soviet state.

The failure of Facing the Wind and Earth to reflect Party policy forced Stalin and the Soviet leadership to the conclusion that censorship and the "political reliability" of individual directors were not enough to discipline the industry. Cinema still lacked coordination with the other channels of propaganda. At the same time, the initiation of forced industrialization and rural collectivization brought additional pressure on the Soviet leaders to intensify the propaganda campaign, particularly on the mass of workers and peasants. For these reasons, the Central Committee of the Communist Party decided late in 1930 to impose an artistic style on Russian cinema. This style was part of the general movement known as socialist realism.

Socialist Realism: Chapayev

Socialist realism can never be precisely defined as an artistic movement because it was intentionally designed to be whatever the Communist Party thought was expedient at a given time. On occasion, socialist realism emphasized the struggle against internal subversion. During the war, socialist realism meant patriotic propaganda; after the war, it centered on anti-imperialism. A scenario writer could be certain that he was following the dictates of socialist realism only if he was avoiding Party criticism.

Despite this lack of an objective definition for socialist realism, several important elements of film-making style remained constant throughout Stalin's lifetime. The early Soviet experiments in expressing historical events and conflicts through advanced editing techniques, lighting and symbolic details were denounced in 1930 as "formalistic intellectual fireworks." Socialist realist films required a clear story line centering on a single individual; there would be no future "storyless" films like Earth or "mass heroes" as in Battle Cruiser Potemkin. Socialist realist motion pictures were to be part of the education of the masses, helping the individual worker and peasant understand how he could build towards a socialist future. Above all, cinema had to remain slavishly responsive to the changing propaganda needs of the Communist Party. In late 1938, a further requirement of socialist

realism--the constant praise of Josef Stalin as an individual--
was introduced.

Immediately after the imposition of socialist realism
as the guiding force of Russian cinema, the number of features produced by Soviet studios each year fell to the lowest
level since 1925. Although Boris Shumyatsky blamed the
transition from silent to sound film production and the difficulties of coordinating the motion picture industry into the
First Five-Year Plan, it is clear that the reduced production
was also due to the fear among writers of working in a politically sensitive area and to Shumyatsky's heavy-handed
mismanagement. The few features which were produced during this transition period, such as Counterplan (1932), co-
directed by Ermler and Yutkevich, were similar in propaganda
technique to the earlier work of Pudovkin. These early socialist realist films centered on the efforts of "New Soviet
Men"--Communist Party members and shock workers--to
complete industrial projects on schedule despite the sabotage
of subversives and foreigners. The propaganda was extremely
ineffective because the plots quickly became predictable and
because the New Soviet Man's complete dedication to industrial production made him a remarkably unattractive hero.
There was no possibility of audience identification with stereotypes completely devoid of human feelings and motivations.

In 1934, the transition from silent film to sound film
production was complete in all major studios, and Shumyatsky
was brought under great pressure to increase the output of
the industry. By this time, however, several older directors,
including Eisenstein, Dovzhenko, Lev Kuleshev and Yakov
Protazanov, had fallen into disfavor, either for political reasons or because of personal conflicts with Shumyatsky.
Young film-makers were therefore given the opportunity to
complete important assignments which normally would have
been reserved to more experienced directors.

Georgi N. and Sergei D. Vasiliev were among the
young film-makers who benefited from this situation. For
Chapayev, they received a larger budget than Pudovkin had
received for his classic Storm over Asia. Their entire
crew was shipped from Leningrad to the scenes of Commander Chapayev's victories, a distance of over a thousand
miles. Both the film-makers of Leningrad and the Party
officials recognized the risks of investing heavily in a work
by two novice directors; nevertheless, it was considered to
be less of a risk than assigning Chapayev to a politically

unreliable director of the Eisenstein-Pudovkin-Dovzhenko generation.

In writing the scenario for the film, the Vasiliev "brothers" (they were not, in fact, related, but the nickname stuck to them for the ten years of their partnership) altered the character of the historical Red commander almost beyond recognition. His deep religious sense, his anarchistic political beliefs and his notorious requisition policies are never mentioned in the film. Nevertheless, the Vasilievs gave "their" Chapayev a highly original, realistic personality. His overwhelming conceit, for example, is revealed in a midnight discussion with his aide:

> 'Commander, do you think you could handle the command of this entire Ural front?'
> 'I think so ... yes, of course.'
> 'And if you were in command of all the armies of Soviet Russia, could you manage it?'
> 'Yes, I could.'
> 'What if you were in command of all the armies of the whole world? What then?'
> 'No, not alone ... I don't know any languages.'

The remainder of the film consists of a series of similar anecdotes which gradually reveal the character of the guerrilla commander. The central conflict of the drama centers on Chapayev's relationship with Furmanov, a Bolshevik political organizer attached to the division against the commander's desires. At first, there is faintly concealed hostility between the two men, and this comes to a climax when Chapayev angrily defends one of his officers who has been found looting a peasant village by the alert Furmanov. Slowly, however, the commissar and the guerrilla leader develop strong bonds of friendship and understanding. As Furmanov discovers the intimate details of Chapayev's character, the audience also learns to accept the illiterate, vulgar egotist as a brilliant charismatic leader and a natural humanitarian. His death, while he is attempting to escape a White ambush by swimming the Ural River, is a universally tragic scene, partly because it is suspenseful (will Chapayev succeed in reaching the other shore in safety?) and partly because the character created by the Vasilievs rises above the propaganda.

It was impossible for the Vasiliev "brothers" to portray Chapayev as a member of the Communist Party. Not only would this have been totally false, but it would also

have removed the initial source of the dramatic conflict with
Furmanov. Instead, the Vasilievs' Chapayev is a Bolshevik
sympathizer who would have joined the Party if he had not
been illiterate and politically ignorant. This distorted image
of Chapayev's politics is revealed in a conversation between
Furmanov and Chapayev, immediately after Chapayev has announced to his cheering troops that "he is for the International." Furmanov takes the commander aside and gently
asks if he "is for the Second or Third":

> 'The Second or Third what?'
> 'There are two Internationals, commander. Are
> you for the Second or the Third?'
> 'I'm for the one I should be for!'
> 'And which is that?'
> 'Which one is Lenin's?'
> 'Lenin is in the Third International, commander.'
> 'Then I'm in the Third International too!'

The enemy is almost never seen in Chapayev, except
in battle sequences and in a sub-plot involving a White colonel and his cossack orderly. The propaganda purpose of
this sub-plot is to contrast the attitude of White officers
towards the common man with Chapayev's treatment of his
men. The White colonel is fond of his orderly and respects
the cossack's loyalty, but remains condescending. When the
orderly's brother, a White cavalryman, is condemned to
death for attempted desertion, the colonel will not stop the
execution. Chapayev, on the other hand, protects his men
from court-martial and invites the lowest soldier in his division "to come and have tea, something to eat" with him in
the evening. The implication is that the counter-revolutionaries, despite their claims of sympathy for the workers and
peasants, lacked the true common touch of the Bolsheviks and
their allies.

A second sub-plot illustrates the role of romance in
the class struggle. Petka, a machine-gunner, attempts to
flirt with Anya, his pupil. Anya continually pushes him
away, saying "You men are all heroes with the girls, but
cowards in the field." She insists that he perform a feat of
bravery, such as capturing a White soldier, before she will
have anything to do with him. Inspired by this challenge,
Petka goes alone on patrol and eventually helps the White
colonel's orderly to desert to Chapayev with valuable information. The romance ends tragically, however, when Petka
is killed with his commander on the banks of the Ural.

The propaganda technique and technical style of Chapayev were evidently derived both from Pudovkin and from early
socialist realism.   As in Storm over Asia, Chapayev depends
primarily on audience identification with individual characters
for its propaganda impact.   The Reds--Petka, Chapayev, etc.
--are heroes endowed with intelligence, courage, dedication,
humor and other positive characteristics.   Their enemies--
looters, defeatists, Whites--are cowardly, callous and cynical
when they are shown as individuals.   The only "virtuous"
enemy is the White colonel--and, in his case, personal courage and concern for his men are balanced by a lack of
warmth, hypocrisy and, above all, by a lack of conviction in
the cause for which he knows he will die.   Thus the Vasilievs'
characters are much more complex than those of Pudovkin;
nevertheless, the basic principle of Reds being all good and
Whites being all villainous remains the central theme.

The socialist realist elements are equally apparent.
The lesson of Chapayev is that a non-Party member can play
a crucial role in the class struggle if he is true to the Party
ideals and responsive to the Party's guidance.   Furmanov's
intervention is described throughout the film as necessary;
without the guidance of the Party as embodied in the political
commissar, Chapayev would supposedly have remained an ineffective, small-scale partisan leader.   This heavy emphasis
on the role of the Communist Party, almost unknown in Soviet films before 1930, is a definitive characteristic of socialist realism.   Other aspects of Chapayev which reflect
early socialist realism are the emphasis on the heroic individual (New Soviet Man) rather than the historic event, the
obvious falsification of history and the importance of long
speeches in clarifying the political message.   The technical
elements of the film--the lack of dramatic editing, the sta-
tionary camerawork, the vast number of "extras" in the cast
and the overbearing musical accompaniment--are also characteristic of socialist realism during this period.

Cinema of the Mediocre

Chapayev was one of the very few artistic and propaganda successes to emerge from the industry during Shumyatsky's management.   Only a few of the young film-makers
promoted out of the cutting rooms and writing staffs to the
position of director had the creative talents of the Vasiliev
"brothers," Yutkevich, Kheifits and Zarkhi.   The remainder,
despite their political orthodoxy, were unable to devise

details of characterization necessary to make the New Soviet
Man interesting and socialist realist films entertaining.

Golden Taiga (1935) is an example of the mediocre
work which characterized the period. Vladimir Schneiderhof,
an inexperienced director, attempted to combine socialist
realism with a Hollywood-style adventure story. The resulting plot reflects the worst aspects of Zhdanov principles and
Hollywood cinema. Golden Taiga starred handsome Andrei
Novoseltsov as a Soviet geologist searching for gold and res-
cuing the heroine from a gang of illegal prospectors. In the
process, Novoseltsov fights various villains barehanded and
makes a speech explaining why the Soviet Union needs gold
for foreign exchange instead of for the bourgeois concepts of
wealth which motivate opportunists. At the climax of the
film, Schneiderhof achieved a small degree of creativity by
contrasting the modern Russia, symbolized by airplanes
fighting a forest fire, with the old ways, symbolized by a
local shaman who started the fire in an attempt to drive the
Soviet explorers away. Despite the drama of this episode,
the general impression received from Golden Taiga is of
wooden characters wordlessly wandering through the wilder-
ness and listlessly fighting each other, interrupted occasionally by an insipid political harangue.

Because it was difficult to depict life in the modern
Soviet Union without being either blatantly hypocritical or
committing "slander," many scenario writers concentrated on
screenplays set during the Russian Revolution and the civil
war which followed. This tendency was particularly satis-
fying to Stalin, who enjoyed watching re-creations of the revolutionary events in which he took an active role. This trend
was also useful from the propaganda point of view. It served
to remind the Soviet people that the Bolsheviks had actively
defended socialism and the homeland from Whites and foreigners. In addition, motion pictures set during the Revolution and the Civil War served as a substitute for actual revolutionary experience for a generation too young to remember
the events as they happened.

Most of the Stalinist films set during the civil war followed a standard pattern represented by Alexander Feinzimmer's Men of the Sea (1937). Men of the Sea supposedly described the defense of the fortress of Kronstadt from a fleet
of British interventionists. It consists of a succession of
ridiculously easy victories against the imperialists, directed
by an infallible Red Navy officer. The British soldiers

retreat from a handful of rifle shots, their landing barges
are torpedoed, their Marines driven from the beaches by a
single round of shells. In one absurd sequence, two broad-
sides from Kronstadt apparently sink half of the British fleet
while the other ships flee without firing a shot in return.
With the enemy easily routed, Men of the Sea ends in the
classic socialist realist style with the Red Banner of Communism flying over Kronstadt and a vast chorus of voices
singing the entire "Internationale."

By the time of the release of Men of the Sea, even
the most stalwart advocates of socialist realism were tired
of the evil war film formula. Official critics, with the co-
vert approval of Zhdanov, complained that the cowardly, inept Whites and foreign interventionists depicted in films discredited the achievements of the Red Army which fought them
and made the problems faced in winning the civil war seem
trivial.   Above all, the victories over the enemy were always
too easy and did not help the Party in its task of explaining
why the Russian people had to make continued sacrifices to
hold counter-revolution at bay.

Beginning in 1937, writers were encouraged to avoid
submitting war film scenarios for consideration. Instead,
the propaganda needs required more films reinterpreting the
official history of the Party in light of recent purges. Mikhail Ilych Romm, a Siberian-born sculptor and writer, was
given the important assignment of filming the revised history
of the October Revolution in 1937, despite the fact that he
was only 13 years old when the Revolution occurred. The
resulting works, Lenin in October (1937) and Lenin in 1918
(1939) emphasized the contributions of Stalin and Dzerzhinski,
first chief of the secret police, while all but eliminating mention of Stalin's disgraced colleagues: Trotsky, Kamenev, and
Zinoviev. Both films were integral parts of the rewriting of
Soviet history to establish a Lenin cult and justify Stalin's
position as the political and ideological successor to Lenin.
They received the widest possible distribution within the
Soviet Union in addition to being exhibited abroad at meetings
of foreign Communist parties. Lenin in 1918 and Lenin in
October firmly established Romm as a politically reliable,
technically capable director and guaranteed a successful ca-
reer for the actor Boris Shchukin in impersonating Lenin.

A similar attempt to rewrite history was made for the
Great Purges of 1938 in a film by Ermler, Great Citizen
(Part I, 1937; Part II, 1939). Despite Stalin's patronage

and its wide distribution, the film was not a success. Great
Citizen lacks drama; the only movement in the film is that
of characters entering rooms, leaving rooms and making
oratorical gestures. The total absence of characterization
and the endless speeches on party discipline, party organization and the formation of workers' committees bored everyone but the most dedicated members of the Party.

A completely different approach was used by Zarkhi
and Kheifits in the direction of Baltic Deputy (1937), a fictionalized biography of Klement Timirazev, aging intellectual
turned Bolshevik. The high quality of the acting, the believable characterizations and the absence of political clichés
made it far more effective as propaganda than the contemporary works of Romm and Ermler. As in Chapayev and
other successful socialist realist films, the directors relied
on details of characterization to make their positive characters attractive and interesting and their villains unsympathetic.
Timirazev in Baltic Deputy is represented by "Polazhayev,"
an aged physicist who defies the abuse of his colleagues to
join the October Revolution. The role of the scholar/revo-
lutionary was played by Nikolai Cherkassov, then 34 years
old and already the most honored Soviet actor.

Baltic Deputy is not a great work, but it has moments
when the characters of Polazhayev and his wife rise above
the scenario. One such moment occurs when the planned
celebration of the physicist's birthday and the publication of
his book is boycotted by his life-long friends and associates
because of his revolutionary politics. The professor and his
wife attempt to console themselves by playing waltz duets on
the piano, but their depression is too great. As his wife
turns from the piano in tears, Polazhayev's mood suddenly
changes and he breaks into a powerful, defiant series of
crescendos.

Unlike other socialist realist films set during the
time of the revolution, Baltic Deputy avoided the falsification
of history for the greater glory of the Stalin regime. Instead, the propaganda message was a generalized statement
that political convictions should be of greater moment to the
individual than personal problems of friendship and career.
Its success in presenting this point lies in the nature of the
Polazhayevs'--Klement Timirazev's--sacrifices. The loss
of friends and of professional reputation were more within
the experience of audiences than the problems of Lenin,
Stalin or barely-remembered Red Army commanders. Zarkhi

and Kheifits permitted the audience to identify with Polazhayev,
while Romm and Ermler demanded respect for their characters.

Aleksandrov and Soviet Musical Comedy

Although socialist realism clearly dominated the Soviet
film industry during Stalin's lifetime, a small number of relatively apolitical musical comedies and light romances were
made each year from 1934 through 1944. These were permitted by the Lenin proportion, which seemed to insist on
the production of at least a few "purely entertainment" films
in addition to the more desirable propaganda works.

Grigori V. Aleksandrov was the first director of Soviet musical comedy films and remained, by far, the most
successful. Born in Sverdlovsk in 1903, Aleksandrov was
already working around theaters and music halls at the age
of nine. In 1922, he met Sergei Eisenstein--then an organizer
of outdoor spectacles--and became his assistant. He remained with Eisenstein for ten years, accompanying him on
his tour of America in the early 1930's, where he was apparently exposed to the early musical spectaculars of Busby
Berkeley. On his return to the Soviet Union, Aleksandrov
accepted a commission to film a musical comedy after Eisenstein, in a fit of artistic temperament, rejected it.

Jolly Fellows: A Jazz Comedy (1934), the result of
Aleksandrov's first attempt as an independent director, is
basically an imitation of the Hollywood style. There is very
little plot; merely a succession of absurd situations involving musicians interrupted by popular songs. Some of the
humor in Jolly Fellows is directed against Russians who had
become wealthy during the NEP and aped Western fads and
fashions. Western clothes, for example, are satirized in
the film when a peasant who is invited to attend a fashionable
party must attend wearing the only formal suit in the village:
an Edwardian costume last worn by a German violinist in
1903. The greed of the NEP bourgeoisie is illustrated when
a fat man sits down to eat a whole pig and is horrified to
see the "dinner" run squealing off the table.

Excepting these minor attempts at social commentary,
Jolly Fellows is essentially slapstick comedy. The jolly
musicians of the title hold a rehearsal in a hearse while a
drunk rises blearily out of the coffin; when their instruments

are runied in the rain, they perform a concert by humming
and imitating the sounds of drums and horns; a herd of assorted animals invades a party, etc. At first, Soviet critics
anticipated the reaction from Zhdanov by denouncing Jolly
Fellows for being "inartistic, often senseless and without
object ... it is uncultured, apolitical empty laughter." They
were quickly silenced when Aleksandrov was unexpectedly
awarded the Order of the Red Banner of Labor. This was
clear evidence that the film had been greatly enjoyed within
the Kremlin.

Aleksandrov subsequently directed nine more comedies
through 1945, most of them similar in style and content to
Jolly Fellows. The continuing patronage of his work, evidently by Stalin, was demonstrated in 1943 when the director
received the much-coveted Stalin Prize, two years before the
brilliant Eisenstein received a similar award. Stalin's apparent preference for musical comedy tempted other Soviet
directors, notably the veteran Ivan A. Pyriev, to work within
the genre. Not one of these imitators was able to produce anything as consistently popular as Aleksandrov's Jolly Fellows,
Circus (1936) or Volga-Volga (1938).

The "Reforms" of 1938

In late 1937, the Soviet Union faced threats from Japan
and Germany. For the first time since 1922, invasion seemed
imminent. Historians are now certain that the internal propaganda channels of the Soviet Union were revitalized in 1938
in preparation for the expected conflict; Stalin realized that
a major effort had to be made to mobilize mass support for
the regime in the face of foreign intervention. The changes
in propaganda content were unusually dramatic in the motion
picture industry.

Seven years of sterile socialist realist films such as
Counterplan and Great Citizen had driven Russian audiences
out of the theaters. The blame for this situation fell upon
Boris Shumyatsky. Shumyatsky knew very little about the
technical details of film-making and had demonstrated that
he knew less about the creation of effective propaganda. As
director of the industry, he perceived his primary missions
as disciplining "overly-intellectual" film-makers and keeping
the budgets of the studios as low as possible. These various
traits brought Shumyatsky into constant conflict with the best
Soviet directors, particularly Sergei Eisenstein. It was

largely through Shumyatsky's efforts that the most experienced
film-makers were "exiled" to classrooms at the State Film
Institutes and to distant studios of Armenia and Central Asia.

Shortly after Christmas, 1937, Shumyatsky was removed from all positions of responsibility. At first, his support for the production of an unusually dull and costly socialist realist version of Treasure Island was given as the reason
for the dismissal; later he was charged with permitting
"savage veteran spies and saboteurs" to infiltrate the studios.
In February, Shumyatsky and most of the remaining Party
members in the industry administration were arrested and
several were executed. At the same time, the administration of the film industry was raised to the semi-ministry
level under the direct supervision of the Council of People's
Commissars. These actions transferred ideological control
of cinema from the Party bureaucrats, who had been responsible for the decline in quality, to the highest echelons of
the government. Stalin himself increased his intervention in
the affairs of Soviet cinema during the following decade,
partly to assume direct responsibility for the propaganda
campaigns and partly out of an egotistical desire to see his
life and personality glorified in films.

An example of this increased intervention is the story
behind the completion of Schors (1939), a film biography of
the Red Military Commander of the Ukraine from 1917 to
1919. Stalin had personally asked Dovzhenko to direct the
film in 1935 as "a Ukrainian Chapayev," but Shumyatsky and
other bureaucrats had created delays, insisting on frequent
revisions of the script and the "temporary" assignment of
Dovzhenko to other projects, such as Aerograd (1937). The
script revisions were considered necessary because the historical Schors' closest associates had been purged as enemies
of the people; according to Zhdanov socialist realism, such
characters could not be depicted as Bolshevik supporters during the civil war. In addition, Dovzhenko's characterization
of Schors as an intellectual irritated Shumyatsky, who apparently believed that no intellectual could be sincerely dedicated
to Communism. Finally, Shumyatsky strongly opposed the
large budget which was being consumed by a director he had
decided was politically unreliable.

The purge of Shumyatsky and Stalin's intervention
ended the major obstacles to the completion of the film.
Dovzhenko quickly replaced all mention of the historical associates of Schors in the script with a rustic, Chapayev-like

character named Batko Bozhenko. Bozhenko, who had never
existed in history, was described as "Deputy Commander" to
Schors and provided the comic relief in the completed motion
picture. The result of Dovzhenko's rewriting was a confused,
uneven work composed of separate scenes filmed throughout
the five years of Schors' production. Nevertheless, Schors
satisfied Stalin and Dovzhenko was reinstated as an honored
Soviet artist for the first time since 1930.

Aleksandr Nevsky and the Historical Spectacle

        Sergei Eisenstein also benefited from Shumyatsky's de-
parture and immediately tested the relative freedom of "relaxed" socialist realism. He chose to devote his first completed work since 1929 to a Russian nationalist theme with
contemporary parallels: the 13th-century struggle between
the Russian city of Novgorod and the Germanic Livonian
Knights. The resulting film, Aleksandr Nevsky (1938) embodied the current Party slogan: "The enemies were beaten,
are being beaten and will be beaten." The slogan applied
both to recent internal purges and to the threat posed by
Germany. Eisenstein's innovation in illustrating the slogan
was the abandonment of the usual socialist realist emphasis
on the defense of the country by the Party in favor of the
historical, patriotic defense of the country by the Russian
people under Prince Nevsky. The innovation reflected growing nationalism among the Soviet leadership.

        Eisenstein's Prince Nevsky was transformed from his-
torical merchant and warlord into a character more acceptable
to the dictates of socialist realism. He is seen in the opening scenes of the film as a peasant-ruler capable of plowing
his own fields as well as leading his subjects. The title
role was played by Nikolai Cherkassov as a man of few words
and many heroic postures. Physical characteristics aside,
Eisenstein's Nevsky could be closely identified with the image
that Stalin wished to create for himself: a strong, ruthless,
but benevolent Russian patriot defending the Russian people
in a time of desperate danger.

        Nevsky's internal enemies in the film are the mer-
chants of Novgorod, representing capitalists and opportunists.
In contrast to the majority of Nevsky's cheerful, smiling subjects, the merchants are depicted as grim, cowardly and un-
patriotic. A noted critic, Parker Tyler, suggests that the
actors chosen to portray the chief merchants intentionally

resemble recently-purged Communist party officials. By
forcibly confiscating money needed for the defense of Novgorod from these class enemies, Eisenstein's Prince Nevsky
demonstrates the need to be ruthless for the good of the
country.

The Germans exist only to be defeated in a famous
battle sequence and are depicted as dehumanized masses of
heavy armor. Their helmets are topped by strange pagan
symbols and the crosses on their capes bear a striking resemblance to swastikas. Of particular interest is Eisenstein's use of massed shields and mounted knights to create
an image of modern tanks advancing into Russia. The Germans' actions reinforce their inhumanity, particularly when
they burn elders of the captured city of Pskov under the
supervision of sorcerer-like Catholic monks.

There is little plot to Nevsky. Prince Aleksandr
rallies the people of Novgorod to the defense of the homeland. Frenzied preparation is followed by a vast battle
scene filmed at great expense with thousands of actors and
gigantic artificial ice flows. At the highpoint of the battle,
Nevsky personally kills the enemy commander and, perched
on a huge rock surrounded by his army, proclaims the day
a victory for Russia.

The film received mixed criticism in the Soviet Union.
Stalin, after seeing Aleksandr Nevsky at his private preview,
is reported to have pounded the director on the back, shouting, "Eisenstein, you are a good Bolshevik!" Stalin's favor
led to Eisenstein's reinstatement in the Party's good graces.
All critics and film historians in the U.S.S.R. were in-
structed to praise the work and its creator. In private,
Eisenstein's colleagues were disappointed. The film's style
was basically conventional; it lacked the drama and realism
of his earlier work. The director remarked bitterly: "I
didn't die at the right time. What a monument would have
been raised to my memory if I had died after Potemkin! I
have made a mess of my own biography." A friend reportedly
asked, "How could you sink so low?"

Despite this criticism, Soviet film-makers immediately
saw the opportunities to escape from conventional socialist
realism with its repetitive emphasis on the role of the Party
in the patriotic historical spectacle. The novelist Aleksei
Tolstoy contributed a screenplay for Peter the Great (1939)
shortly after the release of the Eisenstein film. Eisenstein's

artistic rival, Vsevolod Pudovkin, directed <u>Minin and Pozhar-</u>
<u>sky</u> (1939), a chronicle of the Russian defeat of the Poles
during the 16th century. The nationalist spectacle quickly replaced the civil war drama as the dominant genre of Russian
cinema, partly because of the number of such films produced
and partly because of their enormous budgetary requirements.

Although the patriotic spectacles covered almost every
period of Russian history and featured heroes from every social class, they shared details of theme and characterization.
Inevitably, they centered on the exploits of "The Great Man,"
an infallible leader of unblemished character and patriotism
who personally directs the battle against invaders and internal
enemies. Clearly, "the Great Man" was a stand-in for the
contemporary Stalin. Equally inevitably, the films emphasized the military. The enemy was always a faceless horde,
devoid of humanity, while the Russians were always willing,
cheerful citizen-soldiers united solidly behind the great leader.
The concept of national unity was so important that Pudovkin's
<u>Admiral Nakhimov</u> (1946) was banned for five years because
it depicted revolutionary unrest among Russian sailors during
the Crimean War, a favorite theme during the earlier period
of socialist realism.

Initially, patriotic spectacles appealed only to Russian
nationalism to the extent that a 17th-century Ukrainian patriot,
Bogdan Khmel'nitsky, was shown as wishing union with Russia in his 1941 film biography. During the war, when the
latent nationalism of the Ukrainians was revealed, the smaller
nationalities of the U.S.S.R. were able to see films honoring
their own heroes, such as the Armenian patriot <u>David Bek</u>
(1943) and the Georgian leader <u>Georgi Sadkadzhe</u> (1942 and
1943). The distinguished team of Zarkhi and Kheifits lent
their talents to the direction of a work honoring the founder
of the tiny Mongolian People's Republic, <u>Sukhe Bator Is his</u>
<u>Name</u> (1942). Most historical spectacles, however, remained
within the pattern of emphasizing Russian nationalism and the
defense against European invaders.

Professor Mamlock and Anti-Fascism

Shortly before the outbreak of World War II, Soviet
cinema was enlisted in the anti-fascist propaganda campaign.
This innovation was welcomed by film-makers who wished to
use bourgeois settings but had been prevented by Zhadanov-
type socialist realism. The best known of the anti-fascist

films set in Western Europe was <u>Professor Mamlock</u>, directed
by two Jewish scenario writers, Adolph Minkin and Herbert
Rappaport, in 1938.   In addition to using Germany as a setting, Minkin and Rappaport further tested the "relaxed" socialist realism by making the hero of the title a radical departure from the New Soviet Man.

Basically, <u>Professor Mamlock</u> relates the weakening
opposition of an apolitical, bourgeois surgeon to his son's
Communist activities.   Throughout most of the film, Mamlock
is therefore an anti-hero in socialist realist terms.   The
Jewish surgeon becomes politically aware only after he suf-
fers humiliation by the Nazis.   His conversion to communism
does not save him from assassination while he is making a
defiant anti-Nazi speech to an angry crowd.   Mamlock's sacrifice, however, helps the communist cause by allowing the
more fervently Marxist members of the underground to escape.   Minkin and Rappaport left a false impression that the
German Communist Party was a widespread movement and
the only opposition to the Nazis left in Germany.   This fabrication did not prepare the Russian people for the signing of
a non-aggression pact with Germany in August, 1939.

Several other films with German settings and plots
similar to <u>Professor Mamlock</u> were produced, especially
after the Munich settlement in September, 1938.   Like <u>Mam-
lock, Peat-Bog Soldiers</u> (1938) and <u>The Oppenheim Family</u>
(1939) depicted conditions in Germany in the blackest terms.
These films, along with <u>Aleksandr Nevsky</u>, were withdrawn
from distribution when Molotov and von Ribbentrop signed
their treaty with its secret clauses dividing Eastern Europe
into respective "spheres of influence" and occupation.   Two
years later, the German invasion of Russia brought the anti-
Nazi films and <u>Nevsky</u> back into favor.

Soviet Cinema at War

The German invasion created vast logistical problems
for the Soviet film industry when the feature film studios
were evacuated from Moscow and Leningrad to Armenia and
Central Asia.   The abandoned Mosfilm studio was converted
into headquarters for newsreel production.   Daring cameramen, writers and directors remained at work there while the
front moved up to the suburbs of Moscow.   Feature film
production, however, disappeared for almost a year due to
problems of moving the industry 1,500 miles to the east and
south.

When feature production resumed in the summer of 1942, most of the Party ideologists who had formerly worked in film studios were serving as political commissars in the army. Writers and directors therefore went through a brief period in 1942 when they were expected to make films without propaganda guidance. The result was a strange mixture of widely dissimilar works. Ivan Pyriev abandoned musical comedy to direct Raikom Secretary, a drama emphasizing the Party's direction of the contemporary partisan movement in the pre-1938 socialist realist style. The Vasiliev "brothers," in Defense of Tsaritsyn, depicted young Stalin personally directing the defeat of German interventionist armies on the Volga during the Russian civil war of 1919. The propaganda implication was that Stalin was familiar with German war methods and was using his experience and brilliant tactical mind to direct personally the defense against the new German threat. Defense of Tsaritsyn was released for maximum propaganda effect after the Red Army had trapped the Germans at Stalingrad, the same city which Stalin had defended 24 years before. In contrast to these overt propaganda works was Yuli Raizman's Mashenka, a love story set in the rear of the battlefront.

The Party began to reassert its ideological leadership in the evacuated studios in late 1942. In the propaganda campaign which followed, the role of the Party in directing the resistance was deliberately kept in the background. In addition to the nationalist spectacles and musical comedies, films of the war period centered on the partisan war in the Ukraine. Non-Party men and women were shown leading the patriotic fight against bestial Nazis, who were devoid of human qualities. The partisans were depicted as reacting with equal ferocity in revenge for Nazi atrocities. The Red Army soldiers were all heroes, without human failings, and the films denied the possibility of Russian traitors. Screenplays could depict Russian defeats, but it had to be made clear that the defeats were incorporated in the master strategic plan that led to inevitable victory.

She Defends her Homeland, directed during the winter of 1942-43 by Frederich Ermler, was an early example of the partisan dramas. The film opens with the heroine, Praskovia Lukianova, living a carefree life on her collective farm with her husband and infant son. The invasion is suddenly announced by a menacing roar of bombers overhead. When the Germans arrive, her village is shelled to rubble, her husband killed in battle, her child bayoneted by a

piratical Nazi with a black eye-patch, and it is implied that
Praskovia is raped.   Drifting aimlessly, she wanders into a
camp of dispirited partisans who are retreating before the
German advance.   When the leader of the partisans suggests
further retreat, Praskovia suddenly murders him and insists
that the partisans fight to prevent a repetition of what happened to her and her home.

        The remainder of the film narrates how the partisans
operated under the fanatically spirited leadership of Praskovia
Lukianova.   A crisis is reached when the group hears on the
short-wave of the fall of Moscow, but their leader correctly
orders them not to believe false reports and to set an example for the Russians who are fighting on the home front--the
audience of the film.   In the end, of course, she finds the
one-eyed Nazi who attacked her and kills him with a captured
German tank.

        The title of Ermler's film in Russian invokes the word
"Rodinu," meaning "homeland" rather than the modern concept of "nation" or "state."   Throughout the film, the director includes details which emphasize that the war is a defense
of Russia rather than of the Soviet state.   Before leaving her
house during the evacuation, Praskovia Lukianova sits on a
convenient bench, a traditional Russian ritual insuring luck.
To illustrate tolerance for the old religion, the Communist
organizer of the evacuation permits an old woman to carry a
large ikon with her on the evacuation truck.   Praskovia's
last patriotic speech is filled with references to Russia and
"homeland," but does not include any mention of the Soviet
Union.

        She Defends her Homeland set a pattern for similar
films, but war-time relaxation of socialist realism allowed
directors to exhibit personal styles.   The playwright Boris
Chriskov demonstrated his interest in psychological motivations, impossible with the New Soviet Man, in Invasion (1944).
Instead of being a character endowed with positive virtues,
the hero of Invasion is a bitter former political prisoner who
dies fighting for the homeland despite his alienation from the
State and his family.   The Rainbow (1944) was directed by
Mark Donskoi from the wartime novel in the form of an anti-
Nazi poster transformed into the motion picture medium.
Donskoi detailed the German occupation of a Ukrainian village
with bodies lying unburied in the snow, girls forced to become the Nazis' mistresses, partisans dangling and children
slaughtered.   The climax of the atrocities, in which a

pregnant woman is forced to give birth exposed to the elements and is then bayoneted, is directed with all the skill of a specialist in horror films.   As in She Defends her Homeland, the Russian revenge is almost as brutal, with a woman of the village promising the German prisoners that "The ones who die now will be really lucky."

In late 1944, the feature film studios returned to Moscow and Leningrad while the newsreel personnel followed the front west.   The pattern for war films changed as Party control over the film industry tightened.   The glorification of Stalin, last seen in Defense of Tsaritsyn, slowly reappeared. The role of the Communist Party in defending the country was reasserted in films like Zoya (1944), based on the true story of a Komsomol member who was hanged by the Nazis for acts of sabotage.   The number of feature films declined as feature directors including Dovzhenko and the veteran Yuli Raizman were assigned to documentary work on the front lines.   As the external threat of invasion receded, the need to propagandize the Russian people in support of the defense of Russia declined and a return to the political orthodoxy of pre-1938 socialist realism seemed increasingly desirable to Zhdanov, Stalin and other members of the Party's Politburo.

Conclusions

Under the first fifteen years of Stalin's rule, the key to content in Soviet motion pictures was political expediency. After experiments in coordinating film with other channels of propaganda through the political reliability of individual film-makers failed, Stalin and Zhdanov believed it necessary to impose the principles of socialist realism on the film industry.   Although some of these principles were compromised following the purge of Shumyatsky, film-makers were never able to regain control over the artistic and propaganda content of their work.   Even when films deliberately underplayed the role of the Party in leading the country, it was the Party's decision to enact this policy for specific political reasons.   As the war ended, the bureaucracy, lack of creativity and general stagnation which characterized Stalinist cinema was as much in evidence as during the management of the discredited Shumyatsky.

CHAPTER 5

CINEMA IN THE COLD WAR, 1945-1954

One morning in the early spring of 1946, Mikhail Romm, member of the artistic council of Mosfilm Studios, received a telephone call from the newly-organized Ministry of Cinematography. "Go and see Eisenstein's film," the caller said anxiously, "There's going to be trouble." Romm, a close friend of Eisenstein, had been expecting a warning of this sort. There had been recent rumors that the nearly-completed Ivan the Terrible: Part Two contained material which the Party would denounce as subversive.

Romm, the other members of the artistic council and Eisenstein met later that day for a private screening of the new work. Romm found his worst fears were confirmed. There were clear allusions in Ivan the Terrible: Part Two to similarities between the 17th century tyrant and Stalin and between Ivan's secret police and the NKVD. Eisenstein watched the anxious faces of his colleagues and, smiling ironically, asked: "Is something wrong? Tell me frankly, what's troubling you?" Romm writes of that evening: "Eisenstein's impertinent air, the twinkle in his eye ... showed us that he knew exactly what he was doing, that he had decided to stick his neck out."

Approximately two weeks later, the rebelling director suffered a heart attack at a reception in honor of his winning the Stalin Prize for Ivan the Terrible: Part One, a film released in 1944. In the hospital, Eisenstein was informed that Stalin had viewed Ivan the Terrible: Part Two and had prohibited its public showing. Eisenstein is said to have taken the news calmly; he had expected it. In February, 1947, he met with Stalin and Zhdanov and received permission to refilm Part Two, but his second, fatal heart attack came before the revised work was half-completed. The Ivan the Terrible: Part Two occasionally seen today is the version banned by Stalin in 1946.

Fig. 8. Foreboding shadows hover over the royal wedding
in Ivan the Terrible: Part I. Nikolai Cherkassov
portrays the Tsar, L. Tselikovskaya the Tsarina.
(Source: Private collection)

Starving the Film Industry

Eisenstein's struggle to express himself in Ivan the
Terrible was the only bright moment in the Soviet Union's
cinema during the immediate post-war era. Eisenstein had
long been fascinated by the character of Ivan IV and had received permission to direct a monumental, three-part bio-
graphical film in the early 1940's, shortly after the release
of Aleksandr Nevsky. The first part, released in January,
1945, was considered outstanding among the many nationalist
spectacles of the war years. Nevertheless, it was still tied
stylistically to socialist realism except in the innovative use
of light and shadow to create moods.

Eisenstein's decision to transform the second part of
the film into a veiled attack against Stalin was probably the
result of his disgust with Zhdanov-style socialist realism in
the film industry. The winter of 1945-46 was reminiscent
of the winter of 1928-29, with scores of screenplays being
cancelled by orders of the Party. Articles appeared regularly
in the provincial Soviet press condemning Soviet writers and
scenarists for "ideological emptiness" and adherence to "the
formalistic theory of art for arts' sake ... harmful to the
Soviet people and the Soviet state." Despite these warnings,
the extent of the return to pre-1938 orthodoxy in the film industry was not fully appreciated until the rejection of Ivan
the Terrible: Part Two.

Feature production declined sharply after 1945. This
decline was forced in part by drastic budget cuts and, in
part, by increasingly severe censorship of scenarios. The
devastation in western Russia forced the Soviet government
to concentrate all available capital on reconstruction. With
the immediate threat of invasion temporarily eliminated,
Stalin considered a massive, effective propaganda campaign
in support of the regime unnecessary; money to rebuild the
country was therefore taken from the film industry budget.
Stalin justified this action by insisting that the Soviet studios
produce "quality, not quantity." This "quality" aspect was
enforced by establishing additional "checkpoints" for the review of scenarios before filming. By 1948, every script had
to be cleared by no less than twenty-eight different Party,
studio and Ministry offices before a director was assigned.
Under these pressures, the level of production sank to a
record low level in 1952 when only five features were released.

The Coal Drill as Hero

        A third change in the post-war industry was the shift
in content from war stories to propaganda in support of the
Fourth Five-Year Plan. Stalin wished to weaken the influence
of "war heroes" such as Marshal Zhukov, whose prestige
was increased with every reminder of the sacrifices made by
the Russian people and the Red Army soldier during the recent invasion. At the same time, the unpopular economic
policy needed propaganda support. The new Economic Plan,
with its extreme emphasis on heavy industry and strategic
hardware, had been announced unexpectedly on March 13,
1946, as an answer to American economic pressure. The
response of the Russian people was unusually unenthusiastic.
Unfortunately, with Zhdanov in firm control of the ideological
content of films, the motion picture industry's attempts to
propagandize on behalf of the Fourth Five-Year Plan were
doomed to failure.

        Typical of these propaganda efforts was Donets Miners
(1951), the work of the Ukrainian director Leonid Lukov.
Like Pudovkin, Eisenstein, Yutkevich and other experienced
film-makers, Lukov had fallen into disfavor after the war
over the issue of an uncompleted film. Lukov's downfall
was Great Life: Part Two (1946), a drama about coal miners
which was discovered by the Party to be replete with ideological errors. Lukov's sin in Great Life was apparently
his insistence on complete realism, including the hardships
undergone by the miners in meeting their production quotas.

        Lukov consciously chose to return to the same mater-
ial in Donets Miners in an effort to reinstate himself in the
good graces of the Party. The director was very careful to
avoid his earlier mistake of being realistic. The plot of
Donets Miners reflects this principle: an aged mine worker
retires when a new drill is brought to the coal mine, con-
vinces his son to remain a coal worker instead of moving to
the city and pledges himself to give new workers instruction
based on his years of experience. There are no dramatic
conflicts and no distinguishable personalities. In their place,
Donets Miners offers speeches in praise of progress and
Stalin. The Great Man himself appears in a brief scene,
portrayed by Aleksei Diki, and asks an aide benignly, "What
is that song they're singing in the Donets Basin?" In Lukov's
film, the song is apparently a hymn to the hydraulic drill.
Despite the obvious ineffectiveness of Donets Miners as either
propaganda or entertainment, Lukov's purpose in directing the

film was achieved: he was restored to the Party's favor.

The Five-Year Plan and the New Soviet Man were celebrated in other areas of the Soviet economy. Cavalier of the Gold Star (1951), for example, directed by Yuri Raizman, permitted the audience to compare two collective farmers, Goncharenko and Tutorinov. Tutorinov is a New Soviet Man who organizes a voluntary work detail for the building of a power plant as his special contribution to the fulfillment of the Five-Year Plan. Goncharenko begins by seeking happiness in family life but is convinced by the Party and Tutorinov to sacrifice his free time for the power plant project. Unfortunately for the propaganda impact of Cavalier, Goncharenko the family man was a far more attractive character than Tutorinov with his total commitment to socialist construction. As in Great Citizen, only a Party fanatic finds his political ideals reinforced by Cavalier of the Gold Star.

The Anti-American Campaign

Anti-Americanism in Soviet films had existed since the late 1920's, but it was extremely mild compared to propaganda against England (until 1941), Germany (except for 1939-1941) and Japan. Although America was clearly the major capitalist power in the post-war world, this pattern did not change for almost two years after VE Day. The first major anti-American campaign began in March of 1947 under the direction of Andrei Zhdanov, perhaps as a response to President Truman's program of military aid to Greece and Turkey. The propaganda intensified during the following two years and was diminished only slightly by Zhdanov's death in July, 1948. By the end of the decade, it was a firmly established principle in Soviet film-making that the villains in all stories depicting contemporary events were either American "militarists" or their agents.

The first post-war Soviet film to emphasize anti-American propaganda was Mikhail Romm's 1948 filming of a recent play, The Russian Question. The play and the film seem to be vaguely patterned after a 1925 work by Lev Kuleshev, The Extraordinary Adventures of Mister West in the Land of the Soviets. Like that earlier film, The Russian Question begins with the premise that Americans have been duped by their press into believing that Russia is a backward country whose leaders are preparing war against the West.

Both films involve American visitors to the Soviet Union being unshackled from their prejudices by witnessing the splen-
dors of socialist society.

There are two crucial differences between Mr. West
and The Russian Question. In the 1925 film, the American
press is antagonistic to the Soviet Union out of ignorance:
the Americans honestly believe that Russia is primitive and
hostile. The Russian Question maintains that American press
attacks are part of a capitalist, militarist plot leading to a
new world war. Kuleshev's film is basically optimistic. Mr.
West returns home from the Soviet Union with plans to give
the Senate a truthful account of life in the U.S.S.R. In contrast, Romm's hero, Harry Smith, ends tragically. He loses
his job and his family when he tries to destroy the lie that
the Kremlin is an aggressor. The pessimistic moral of The
Russian Question is clearly that the American people, misled
by their Machiavellian leaders, are destined to invade the
peace-loving Soviet Union.

Romm's success with The Russian Question coerced
other directors into participating in the anti-American campaign out of fear of being identified with the ideological opposition. Abram Room, for example, a respected director of
Dovzhenko's and Protazanov's generation, gave the Soviet film
industry Court of Honor (1948), an unusually vicious attack on
Russian scientists who wished to share their discoveries with
the West. Alexander Feinzimmer, the inept director of Men
of the Sea, was recalled to the studios to film They Have a
Homeland (1950), which accused the Americans of keeping
Russian child prisoners-of-war as virtual slaves in Germany
and the United States. At this point, parallels between the
Nazis and the Americans were considered to be the most effective propaganda technique. Feinzimmer, for example, depicts the Nazis dragging helpless children into slavery as a
prologue, then concludes They Have a Homeland with the
identical episode, using American in place of German soldiers.

The ultimate in vilification of the United States was
another work by Romm, Secret Mission (1950). The film
opens with the British and Americans fleeing in the Battle
of the Bulge while the Red Army attacks German positions
on the Elbe to take pressure off their beleaguered allies.
As soon as the cowardly Allied armies are saved, a nego-
tiating team of Americans flies in secret to Berlin to meet
with Nazi officers. There, quaking with fear from the Russian shelling in the background, the Americans are thanked

by the Germans for their "cooperation" during the war in supplying German armies on the Eastern Front with needed supplies. The Americans' attempt to negotiate a separate peace, however, is foiled by an early Russian assault on Berlin. The Americans then fly to the Balkans where they attempt to organize pro-Nazi, anti-Soviet resistance forces directed against Red Army "liberating" troops. Again, the American negotiators are defeated in their purpose by prompt Soviet action.

When Secret Mission was released, reviews and publicity for the film emphasized the fact that "it is a fictionalized documentary, based on historic events." Topical events such as American discussions on German rearmament and early West German demands for independence were cited as evidence that the film was a historical record of American-Nazi collaboration.

The attacks on America and Western culture were followed logically by the glorification of Russian culture. Stalin, Zhdanov and other Soviet leaders informed the Russian intellectuals that they had been wrong to think that the great artistic and scientific achievements of recent times had been European. The result of this policy in the film industry was a series of postwar film biographies of great Russians such as Ivan Pavlov (1949), the father of Russian psychology; Aleksandr Popov (1950), the supposed inventor of the radio; Zhukovski (1950), the supposed inventor of the airplane; and Dzhambul (1952), a recently deceased Kazakh poet who had been extremely vocal in his praise for Stalin throughout his lifetime. The subjects of these biographies were carefully chosen from the ranks of dead Russian intellectuals to insure their acceptability to the regime. The plots were also regimented: invariably, the hero fought the indifference of his Tsarist or bourgeois contemporaries, defended his work from the plotting of foreigners and predicted that future generations would recognize his patriotism and his greatness. Attempts to deviate from this pattern, as in Dovzhenko's last feature, Life in Bloom (1949), were met with the opposition of the Motion Picture Ministry. In filming the life of I. V. Michurin, the founder of Russian genetics, the Ukrainian director was accused of violating socialist realism by his failure to place the scientist "in his social and political context."

The Enshrined Stalin

The five years from the death of Zhdanov in 1948 until the death of Stalin in 1953 mark the highpoint of the "cult of Stalin" in Russian politics and culture. After removing the Red Army officers in 1945, Stalin attempted to invest himself with their charismatic leadership. Since he was personally totally lacking in charisma, the mass media of the Soviet Union was used continuously to project an image of the dictator as the greatest ideologist, military leader, economic planner and cultural critic in history. In addition, the Stalin myth promulgated in the U.S.S.R. during his lifetime made the Great Man a warm, benign personality, patient with his enemies and especially kind to children and old people.

Motion pictures featuring the character of the dictator usually starred either Aleksei Diki or Mikhail Gelovani, both of whom had developed Stalin "masks" acceptable to the original. During the last years of Stalin's lifetime, Diki played the character dressed in gleaming white, without the tiny smallpox scars that marred Stalin's face.

The best-known of the monumental motion picture poems in praise of Stalin is Battle of Stalingrad (1949). In directing the film, Vladimir Petrov combined documentary footage with fictional scenes to create a feature that looked like history. Despite the title, the film shows the fighting at Stalingrad in the winter of 1942-1943 only sporadically. Most of the action is divided between Hitler's underground bunker and the marbled corridors of the Kremlin, where Stalin is shown directing the battle from his office.

The propaganda emphasis in Battle of Stalingrad is on the contrast between the two dictators. Petrov depicts Hitler as a hysterical madman, impervious to the casualties that he is creating for the greater glory of the Reich. Stalin, on the other hand, is calm, detached, benevolent and humane, taking time out from his military planning to chat with a Kremlin gardener. Lighting, costumes and sets are used to underscore these differences. The ranting Hitler is always shown in dark uniforms, surrounded by his conspiring staff in the dark, stuffy rooms of the bunker. (In fact, Hitler operated out of the idyllic forest retreat of Wolf's Lair during the Stalingrad campaign.) Stalin is costumed in the inevitable white uniform, surrounded by the luxury of the Kremlin and its grounds. His only companion during the planning of the battle is Marshal Voroshilov, who appears, according to one critic, "in order to save Stalin the indignity of talking to himself."

Mikhail E. Chiaureli, a fellow countryman of Stalin from Georgia, directed The Fall of Berlin (1950) in a similar style, integrating newsreel footage of the event with staged material filmed with newsreel cameras. After Stalin's death, this particular "artistic documentary" came under heavy attack from Khrushchev. Recalling the details of The Fall of Berlin, Khrushchev demanded, "Where are the contributions of the Red Army marshals, the Politburo, the strategic planners?" In the film, Stalin is depicted as personally making almost every military decision while army officers praise his inspiration and genius to the exclusion of any credit for their own contributions.

Chiaureli completely destroyed truth in the final episode of The Fall of Berlin in which Stalin lands at Tempelhof Airport surrounded by ecstatic "liberated" Germans. In history, Stalin's arrival in Berlin was delayed until July, 1945, a few days before the Potsdam conference. There were no crowds to welcome him, only a small army of security troops provided for his protection. In 1950, however, Stalin and his advisers had committed themselves to the establishment of the Communist-dominated German Democratic Republic in the Soviet sector of occupied Germany. For this reason, it was necessary for propaganda purposes that the East Germans "welcome" their Russian liberators in the film as their first step towards socialism.

The near-deification of Stalin in Soviet films of the late 1940's and early 1950's was one of the worst failures in Soviet propaganda. A portion of the movie-going audience accepted the image which Stalin wished to project. This success, however, did more harm than good. Stalin came to believe that this minority represented the attitude of the Soviet population as a whole. Khrushchev said of the situation that "Artists and writers made films which were full of lies that would please Stalin, and Stalin came to believe these lies." The members of the Party realized that the campaign to glorify Stalin was leading toward the establishment of one-man dictatorship in which they would not be needed. Thus, the propaganda campaign to increase Stalin's prestige only succeeded in alienating him from the majority of the population and the Party's highest echelons.

Socialist Realism For Export

The reassertion of pre-1938 socialist realist principles
in motion pictures was not limited to the Soviet Union.
Wherever the Red Army conquered territory from the Nazis,
Zhdanov-trained ideologists soon followed, beginning a campaign of persecution of non-Communist intellectuals that eventually led to a Soviet-dominated Eastern Europe. Under Russian occupation, the subordination of Eastern European studios
to Soviet interests proceeded rapidly.

There were three models for Communist take-over of
the national studios of Eastern Europe. In Poland and Yugoslavia, many of the film directors had been Communists or
Communist-sympathizers during the war, serving with com-
bat groups as newsreel cameramen. When the war ended,
the Polish Army Film Command and the Partisan Newsreel
Units of Yugoslavia, both under firm Stalinist political control, moved into the studios and immediately assumed administrative responsibilities for the national industries. In both
countries, the film industry and the film distribution services
were nationalized by late 1945 and placed under the authority
of the Ministry of Information.

Content of Polish and Yugoslav films in the immediate
post-war period reflected the traumatic experiences of the
war years. When feature production was reinstituted in Polish studios in 1947-48, almost all works depicted the suffering of the Polish people under the Nazis. Leonard Buckow-
ski's Forbidden Songs (1947), an extremely realistic presentation of everyday life in occupied Warsaw remains the second most popular film in Polish history, having been seen
by approximately 14 million people. Wanda Jakubowska and
Alexander Ford attacked specific areas of Nazi policy in The
Last Stage and Border Street (both 1948). Jakubowska's experiences as a concentration camp inmate and Ford's sympathy for the massacred fellow Jews of the Warsaw ghetto
are clearly seen in these works, giving them an eloquence
unknown elsewhere in Eastern European cinema during this
period.

In Bulgaria, Rumania and Albania, where national film
industries had not been well-established before the war, film
distribution was immediately placed under Communist political supervision. This action guaranteed that Soviet films
alone would be shown in the three Balkan states. After Communist governments were established, film studios were

Fig. 9. _Border Street_, a Polish anti-Nazi film of the late 1940s. (Source: Film Polski)

Fig. 10. Nazis invade the ghetto in <u>Border Street</u>. (Source: Film Polski)

constructed, first to provide dubbing facilities for the Russian
imports and later to begin small-scale local production. In
all three cases, aspiring directors and actors were sent to
the Soviet State Film Institutes, after being carefully screened
for political reliability. At the Institutes, they were given
large doses of ideological indoctrination along with their training in socialist realist film techniques. These procedures
were highly successful; the national cinemas of Bulgaria,
Rumania and Albania remain dominated by the early, Stalinist-
educated film-makers. Consequently, the productions of the
three Balkan states are the most orthodox in their socialist
realist style.

   The early work of the Bulgarian studios is similar in
content, theme and production values to the initial post-war
films of Poland, Yugoslavia, Albania and Rumania. Sergei
D. Vasiliev, the Russian co-director of Chapayev, was "lent"
to the Bulgarian studios to make Heroes of the Shipka (1948)
and to assist in the development of the Bulgarian film industry along Soviet lines. Heroes of the Shipka, depicting how
a Russian army liberated Bulgaria from Turkish occupation in
the 19th century, was part of the "Russification campaign"
that appeared throughout Eastern Europe during Stalin's lifetime. The object of this campaign, which also included the
exclusive use of Russian-made motion pictures in Eastern
European theaters, was to convince the peoples of the occupied areas that Russian culture, science, political aspirations
and friendship were superior to anything the West had to offer. As a further aid in the Russification campaign in Bulgaria, Soviet studios sent Bulgarian-language versions of anti-
American films to Sofia for distribution almost as soon as
they were completed in Russian.

   The first features to be produced independently in Bulgaria were also connected with the Russification campaign.
The first film to be produced solely by Bulgarians was Ivan
Suzanin (1951), a motion picture record of the performance
of an opera by the Russian composer Glinka. Later films,
such as Danka (1952), attempted to be more orthodox than
the Soviet works by "depicting the struggle of the working
class, led by the Bulgarian Communist Party, against capitalist exploitation and Nazi occupation, as well as the victory
over the odious bloodied fascist dictatorship and the establishment of peoples' rule."

   In Hungary and Czechoslovakia, both Communist political rule and the control of the film industry by the Communist

Fig. 11. The making of a Bulgarian revolutionary in <u>Danka</u>. (Source: Bulgarofilm)

Fig. 12. Pre-war exploitation of the workers in <u>Danka</u>. (Source: Bulgarofilm)

Party were established far more slowly. Nationalization of the industry was given high priority: in Czechoslovakia, the studios were the first private enterprises to be placed under government authority. Nationalization of the film industry in Hungary was not accomplished until March, 1948, but bourgeois and nationalist directors such as Akos Rathonyi and Geza von Radvanyi fled from the persecution of non-Communist intellectuals shortly after the war. Other major directors, including Bela Gaal and Bela Balogh, had died before the Red Army occupation. Only a handful of film-makers, notably Zoltan Fabri, remained active after the nationalization.

In Czechoslovakia, the task of removing the politically unreliable pre-war film industry personnel was based on wartime activities. Many Czech film-makers were killed by the Nazis as nationalist intellectuals. Most of those who survived were condemned as collaborators and were therefore unable to work under the anti-fascist laws of the post-war regime. The remaining directors and actors agreed to submit to the supervision of Communist Party officials in order to keep their jobs. By 1948, both Hungary and Czechoslovakia had achieved a level of censorship equal to that already existing in the post-war Soviet Union.

Film distribution in Czechoslovakia, Hungary and Poland remained relatively free of Party control until late 1948. As a result of this liberal policy, the audiences of these countries were able to compare Soviet, socialist realist films with Western imports. It was quickly apparent that Eastern European audiences preferred Hollywood productions to the works of the Zhdanov-dominated Russian studios.

Local productions, particularly in Hungary, initially used pre-war styles and themes. Historical spectacles and costume dramas continued to be produced in Budapest until the nationalization was complete. Afterwards, the Hungarian and Czech studios found their budgets all but eliminated unless they produced Russian classics and socialist realist works in the style of Cavalier of the Gold Star. The local audiences and intellectuals found the "progressive improvements" completely unpalatable. A popular Hungarian joke of the early 1950's told the story of a man suffering from overwork, stress and depression, whose doctor advised him to go to the movies. The doctor warns him: "But for God's sake don't go to Hungarian movies! They'll only make you worse." It was a bitter reflection from people who had been

used to the entertaining, extravagant musicals of the 1930's
and the glossy Western imports of the post-war years.

Conclusions

The reasons for the return to orthodox socialist realism lie in Stalin's desire to "cleanse" his country of the liberal influences created by war-time conditions and by the desire to achieve certain propaganda goals.   These goals--sup-
port for the Fourth Five-Year Plan, anti-Americanism and
the creation of a Stalin myth to guarantee the dictator's personal power--were to prove elusive because of the artistic
bankruptcy of socialist realism as an effective means of propaganda.   Inept directors and film-makers such as Feinzimmer
thrived in the intellectual climate created by Zhdanov, while
the best of the Soviet directors including Eisenstein, Pudovkin,
Dovzhenko and Yutkevich fell into decline.   The only capable
directors who could remain active were those like Romm and
Lukov who made a conscious decision to sacrifice their talents to political expediency.

In the other countries of Eastern Europe, the Communist parties were ordered to model their new societies, including the local film industries, after the example set by the
Soviet Union.   As a result, the relative creativity and national
feeling expressed in the works of pre-war Eastern European
directors were lost in the post-war "Russification campaign."
The rate of feature production fell throughout the region due
to increased censorship and budgets limited by the fiscal
needs of reconstruction.   One Czech film critic pensively remarked that "the times during the German occupation were
maybe not so bad as the years just after the Red Army came
through."

CHAPTER 6

SOVIET CINEMA SINCE STALIN, 1954-1971

Stalin died in February, 1953. He was one of the
few surviving original Bolsheviks; his successors, Khrushchev and Malenkov, had both joined the Communist Party
after the October Revolution. Although they lacked a definitive policy on the arts, Khrushchev and Malenkov agreed that
Zhdanovist socialist realism accomplished little for the Soviet
state. Some change in the direction of liberalization was
clearly necessary.

This liberalization did not occur immediately after
Stalin's death, for several reasons. First, Stalin's death
coincided with the death, retirement or exile of the handful
of Russian directors who had been active before the era of
socialist realism. Pudovkin, for example, died in the summer of 1953, and this loss was followed closely by Dovzhenko's
long, fatal illness. Yutkevich was assigned as advisor to the
poverty-stricken Albanian national film industry. Lev Kuleshev, the eldest and most experienced Russian director, remained in semi-retirement as administrative director of the
Moscow State Film Institute.

A second reason for the delay in liberalization, beyond
the physical loss of qualified personnel, was political. The
experienced directors who had lived through the worst excesses of Stalinism, such as Romm, Ermler, and Sergei D.
Vasiliev, had been conditioned to avoid innovation for fear of
reprisals. The concept that the Stalinist system of repression had died with Stalin was not popular among Russian intellectuals until Khrushchev denounced the late dictator at the
20th Party Congress in 1956.

A third factor was uncertainty as to the attitude of
Stalin's successors towards the arts. As they jockeyed for
supreme power, Khrushchev and Malenkov shifted their ideologies to fit their purposes, sometimes appearing as

Stalinists and sometimes as liberals. Artistic innovation in films might offend one of the two contestants for leadership, and the intellectuals of the film industry were unwilling to risk their careers by choosing the wrong side in a political quarrel.

Despite these problems, change was inevitable in both the style and content of Russian motion pictures. Neither Malenkov nor Khrushchev wanted to perpetuate the "Stalin myth." This policy was communicated to the film-makers by the gradual withdrawal from circulation of those films which featured the near-deified character of Stalin. To replace the work of the post-war years, film-makers were encouraged to work with filmed versions of Russian and foreign classic works. This was considered the safest category of films during the politically hectic years of the mid-1950's. In effect, Malenkov and Khrushchev avoided the use of film as propaganda for fear that it might be used as a political weapon to their opponent's advantage.

Classics into Film: Shakespeare as a Russian

The first of the Russian classics to be made into film during the post-Stalin era was the opera Boris Godunov by the late 19th-century composer Mussorgsky. Directed in 1954 by a newcomer, Vera Stroyeva, the lavish production avoided the usual practice of simply filming a performance of the opera. Stroyeva placed the company of the Bolshoi Theater amidst a great throng of "extras" on location in country inns, Kremlin palaces and massive outdoor sets. In effect, Stroyeva was experimenting with the concept of the "mass hero" which was perfected by Eisenstein in the 1920's and banned as formalistic in the 1930's. It was a major step towards liberalization--but only in the style, not the content, of motion pictures. Other Russian classics also filmed in 1954, such as Vladimir Petrov's The Inspector General, remained simply filmed performances. Although The Inspector General could not have been made during Zhdanov's lifetime because the Stalinist fanatic would have imagined the satire to be secretly directed against Communist bureaucracy, it must be classified as a socialist realist work in its stylistic elements.

The vogue for foreign classics began in 1955 with the filming of Shakespeare's Othello by Yutkevich. Yutkevich's choice of the play is not surprising; Roger Manvell notes

that "It is with Shakespearian tragedy ... that English writing
has come closest to the taste of the Russian intelligentsia."
The director had thought about making a motion picture adaptation of the play as early as the mid-1930's, but had been
blocked by the dictates of socialist realism. When Orson
Welles' Othello (1952) won a Cannes Film Festival award,
Yutkevich again decided to abandon hopes of beginning the
Othello project. After seeing the Welles version, he changed
his mind again. Welles had made Othello a film of intense
violence, beginning with the dead bodies of Othello and Desdemona carried in their coffins. Yutkevich disliked this interpretation and began working on a possible scenario. In
effect, he was motivated by the desire to produce a "better,"
more "artistic" version than the Western production.

     Yutkevich's Othello is faithful to the original play in
its dialogue, but the director changed the settings to make
the best possible use of the Yalta seacoast where it was
filmed. (Commonweal magazine mistakenly thought it had
been filmed in Venice and Cyprus, where the action of the
play takes place.) The Russian film is far more lyrical and
romantic than the Western versions. Instead of opening with
the abduction of the heroine, as in the original play, Yutkevich begins his Othello with Desdemona's daydreams of the
adventurous life of her lover. The character of Othello, as
portrayed by Sergei Bondarchuk, had less psychological motivation than that of Western Othellos.

     The greatest difference between the Yutkevich Othello
and Western productions is in theme. Welles and other
European directors conceive of the play as a drama of jealousy, with the Moor of Venice a man "who loved not wisely
but too well." Yutkevich limited the scenes between Desdemona and her husband; she is more often seen by herself
than with Othello. Instead, the Russian version subtly emphasizes the role of Othello as a leader betrayed by his
trusted subordinate. This theme of misplaced trust is peculiarly Russian, as seen in such earlier films as Ivan the
Terrible and Peter the Great. The change of emphasis, accomplished through the extensive use of close-ups during con-
frontations between Iago and Othello and through symbolic settings, does not detract from the Shakespearian content of the
film. Instead, the "Russification" of Othello creates a fresh
viewpoint for audiences familiar with Western productions.

     The popularity of Yutkevich's Othello and the praise
of the official press encouraged other Soviet directors to work

with Shakespearian material. Twelfth Night (1956), directed
by Yakov Fried, a relative unknown, was a critical failure.
Fried de-emphasized the dialogue, relying for comic effect
on gross characterizations and slapstick.

A colleague of Yutkevich from the late 1920's, Grigori
Mikhailovich Kozintsev, directed a brilliantly artistic Hamlet
in 1963-64.   Like Yutkevich, Kozintsev remained faithful to
the Shakespearian text, but was able to change the theme of
the story through details not included in the play.   The Russian Hamlet is, in effect, a drama centering on the struggle
of a political rebel, Hamlet, to overcome the politically re-
pressive regime of his uncle, the usurper.   Kozintsev depicts life at Elsinore as a Medieval prototype for Stalinist
society.   Spies follow Hamlet, taking notes of his actions;
Laertes attempts a palace revolution when he learns of his
father's death.   The characters in the Russian Hamlet are
all either manipulators, such as Hamlet, the king and the
opportunistic Polonius, or pawns in the struggle for political
power, such as Ophelia.   Thus, without departing from the
text, Kozintsev succeeded in directing a Shakespearian film
about Stalinism.

Attacking Stalinism: The Second World War Revisited

The differences between the apolitical Othello of 1955
and the anti-Stalinist Hamlet of 1963-64 underscore the primary change which occurred in the intellectual climate during
the intervening years.   By the end of the Khrushchev era,
Soviet film-makers had regained a large measure of the control over the content of their films which they had lost under
Stalin.   They still could not criticize the politics of contemporary society;   on the other hand, they could attack the
flaws in Soviet society that existed under Stalin.   This freedom was undoubtedly granted by the Soviet leaders as part
of their campaign to remove the former dictator from his
pedestal.   The right to attack Stalinism--and, indirectly,
Stalin--was useful primarily because it underscored the "improvements" made by Stalin's successors.   Secondarily, criticism of life under Stalin provided an outlet for the tensions
created by the inability of Russian intellectuals to attack
their contemporary problems.

The first step in destroying the Stalin myth, after removing from circulation films which overpraised him, was
the destruction of the picture of Stalin as the great military

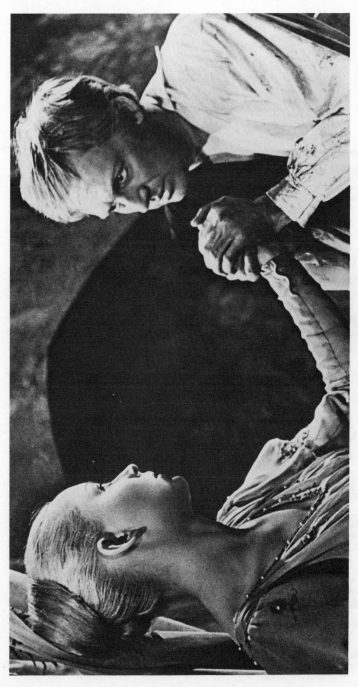

Fig. 13. Anastasia Vertinskaya as Ophelia, and Innokenti Smoktunovski as a mature Soviet Hamlet. (Source: Iskusstvo)

Fig. 14. The intrigue-ridden royal family of the Soviet Hamlet. (Source: Iskusstvo)

genius of World War II. This was accomplished by a series
of films which presented the war years in far more realistic
terms than in the pompous semi-documentaries popular during
the early 1950's. The directors responsible for the "humanistic" approach to Soviet war films were Grigori Naumovich
Chukrai and Mikhail Konstantinovich Kalatozov.

Kalatozov represents the second generation of Soviet
directors, brought into the industry in 1929 during the period
of transition to socialist realism. Kalatozov was involved in
a series of minor works until 1950 when, at the age of 47,
he finally directed an important film, Conspiracy of the
Doomed. This feature was part of the anti-American campaign, depicting the Vatican involved in an imperialist conspiracy to take over Poland. Despite the film's notorious
unpopularity among the people of Eastern Europe, Kalatozov
was awarded a Stalin Prize for his efforts. The unfortunate
director became closely identified with the worst aspects of
post-war socialist realism as a result of his participation in
Conspiracy of the Doomed.

Kalatozov's next film was The Cranes Are Flying
(1957), a work designed to show that he had severed his former connections with Stalinism. In terms of style, The
Cranes Are Flying was a return to the techniques of Soviet
silent films. Kalatozov used elements which would have been
condemned as "formalistic" under Zhdanov: close-ups of
marching feet, montage images of war based on Eisenstein's
formerly-forbidden editing techniques. Although these stylistic elements would not have appeared unusual in a film produced in the West, they represented a major break from the
socialist realist techniques of directing war films.

The plot and theme of The Cranes Are Flying were
almost as innovative as its style. Kalatozov wished to produce a "little drama" of the Second World War similar to
those produced during the brief period of "relaxed" socialist
realism in 1942-43. The story involves believable, realistic
characters: Boris, a patriotic young man; his lover,
Veronica; Mark, a selfish pianist who seduces Veronica
while Boris is serving in the army. Ashamed of her conduct, Veronica agrees to marry Mark. At the same instant,
Boris dies in battle, his final thoughts a montage vision of
his unfaithful girl back home. Veronica eventually tires of
her life with the egocentric artist and leaves him, expecting
to be reunited with Boris. When she learns of his death
from another soldier, she decides to break completely with
the past and live for the future.

The Cranes Are Flying is important because it represents a break with the socialist realist characterization of all
people as great heroes or black-hearted villains.   Veronica
is complex in her motivations and her emotions.   Her wartime tragedy is unlike those of earlier World War II heroines
because it does not result directly from the invasion.   Instead, her unhappiness is derived from her own weaknesses,
compounded by the loss of the stabilizing influence of her
parents in a bombing raid.   In other respects, however, The
Cranes Are Flying is still tied to socialist realism.   The
character of Mark, for example, is unrelievedly evil.   The
optimistic ending also strikes a jarring note in the otherwise
realistic drama.   Apparently, the habits of a lifetime of directing films under Stalinism were difficult to break.

Grigori Chukhrai, on the other hand, represents the
post-war generation of Soviet directors.   Born in 1921, his
youth and education were almost ideal from the Communist
viewpoint.   After graduation from high school in 1939, Chukhrai joined the army, where he saw action against the Finns
and the Germans.   In 1944, he became a member of the
Communist Party, which proved useful in obtaining entrance
to the Moscow State Film Institute after the war.   Despite
this admirable record, seven years passed after his graduation from the Institute before he was assigned to direct a
feature film.   This delay was created primarily by the cut-
back in feature film production during the early 1950's.

For his first feature, Chukhrai directed a remake of
a 1927 Soviet silent film set during the Russian civil war,
The Forty-First.   Chukhrai's 1956 version changed the emphasis in the story from the political to the romantic, as
well as adding the benefits of spoken dialogue and a sweeping
musical score.   As in the original, the heroine of Chukhrai's
The Forty-First is a fanatic Bolshevik with an impressive
record of forty White victims.   While she is escorting a
White prisoner, the two enemies become shipwrecked together
on a tiny island.   Chukhrai's main divergence from the silent
version is his treatment of the growing love between the
stranded antagonists.   The original The Forty-First passed
quickly over the romance, in order to emphasize the Bolshevik's dedication to her duty.   Chukhrai directed the same
episode at a leisurely pace, emphasizing its romantic aspects.
In a brief, important sequence, the lovers are seen in sil-
houette, their uniforms invisible against the background of
bounding surf and blazing Asian sky.   At the climax, when
the girl murders her lover to prevent the officer from

returning to his unit, it is the gesture of a human being who
has been overtrained to kill rather than the result of devotion
to a cause. Chukhrai succeeded in cleverly altering the motivations of the two characters to achieve a more humanistic,
more realistic point of view.

Chukhrai's second feature, Ballad of a Soldier (1960),
is set during the German invasion. The "story" consists of
a series of anecdotal encounters between a young soldier trying to reach his home on a ten-day pass and the assorted
people he meets on the home front. Chukhrai begins the
narration by depicting the soldier's sole act of heroism as
the instinctive response of a frightened boy being chased by
an enemy tank. He is equally terrified when confronting his
own general in order to request a leave.

The soldier, who remains nameless throughout the
film, first encounters a troop of men on their way to the
battlefront. They first delay him by asking naive questions
about the fighting and then insist, over their sergeant's ob-
jections, that he take their soap ration as a present to the
wife of one of their comrades. On the trains, he meets a
legless veteran who is afraid to return to his wife and an
unscrupulous train guard who demands a bribe before allowing him to ride in a freight car. A young girl jumps into
the car with him and is terrified that he might be a rapist.
This brief encounter develops into an innocent romantic attachment which ends when she leaves him to catch another
train, but promises to remain "his girl" until they can meet
after the war.

The most poignant of the episodes occurs when the
soldier and the girl attempt to deliver the soap ration. They
find the house bombed and the unknown soldier's wife living
with another man. Furious at the unfaithfulness of the wife
of a man he barely knows, the young soldier gives the soap
to the man's parents, who are living with other homeless
families in a gymnasium. They delay him further, desperately asking after their son in the mistaken belief that their
visitor serves in the same unit. The young soldier hesitates
and then tells them of the popularity and heroism of the man
who asked him to deliver the soap, knowing that this is what
they need to hear.

The final anecdote is the soldier's homecoming, a
confused encounter spent searching for his mother in their
tiny village. When they meet, he has only time enough to

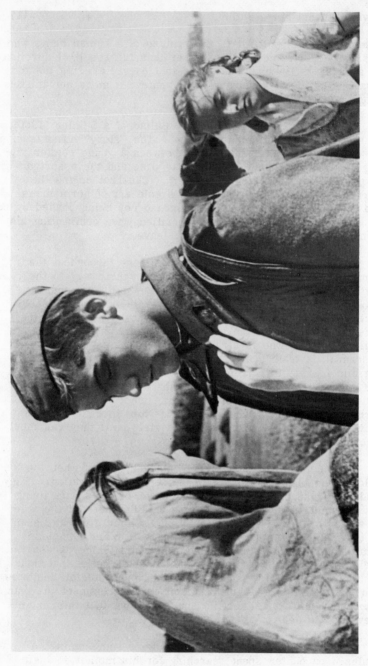

Fig. 15. V. Ivashov as the doomed private in <u>Ballad of a Soldier</u>. (Source: Iskusstvo)

embrace her before he must begin his return to the front.
Chukhrai ends the film with a vision of the mother standing
in the road, watching a truck take her son back to the war,
while the narrator informs the audience that she was never
to see him again.

The essential point of Chukhrai's Ballad of a Soldier
is that it expressed the tragedy of the war on the simplest
level--the misfortunes faced by isolated individuals. There
are no important figures or major battles; Stalin is not mentioned once and the soldier's general is not named. Unlike
those of The Cranes Are Flying, none of Chukhrai's characters is wholly good or evil. Even the unfaithful wife, who
is depicted as being unhappy in her betrayal, unsuccessfully
pleads for understanding from the soldier, telling him sadly
that "he is too young to understand." The truth of her statement is demonstrated in the next scene when the soldier com-
promises his principles by pretending to be a comrade of the
son of the old couple in the gymnasium. In this way, relying mainly on characterization, Chukhrai destroys the myth
that the Soviet people during the Second World War were all
either virtuous patriots or traitors. His Ballad of a Soldier
represents the clearest break with the socialist realist principles of the 1930's and 1940's.

The humanistic characterizations developed by Kalatozov and Chukhrai for their wartime dramas met with widespread approval, both in the Soviet Union and abroad. The
Cranes Are Flying won first prize at the 1957 Cannes Film
Festival, while Ballad of a Soldier won an Academy Award
nomination for Best Foreign Film. Responding to public favor, Sergei Bondarchuk, an actor noted for his portrayal of
Tutorinov in Cavalier of the Gold Star and the title role in
the biographic film Taras Shevchenko (1951), made his direc-
torial debut in 1959 with yet another World War II drama,
Fate of a Man. Bondarchuk also played the central role of
an escaped Russian prisoner-of-war whose despair at the
loss of his family is conquered by an encounter with an or-
phaned boy.

Classical Humanism: Chekhov and Dostoyevsky

A second contributing factor to the appearance of humanism in Soviet films of the early 1960's was a vogue for
motion picture adaptations of classic Russian short stories.
The first of these, a 1955 adaptation of Chekhov's story,

"The Grasshopper," revealed a sentimental attachment for
19th-century Russia among educated, urban audiences. Since
Chekhov is clearly a Russian author and therefore acceptable
as part of the Russian cultural tradition praised by the Soviet
government, this nostalgia could be safely exploited. The result has been a flood of costume dramas based on 19th-cen-
tury Russian classics.

Lady with a Dog (1960) is fairly typical of this genre.
Iosif Kheifits, the ageless co-director of Facing the Wind
(1930), literally translated the short story by Chekhov into
the film medium, using extensive panoramas of the Yalta
setting which has not changed greatly since Chekhov's era.
The plot is extremely simple: a bank official and a young
woman, vacationing away from their respective marriages,
meet in Yalta and fall in love. They part, agreeing to meet
again the following year. The central action of the film occurs years after their initial meeting, when they have realized that their love for each other will always be expressed
in brief, illicit encounters. The history of their affair is
reflected in idyllic flashbacks, interrupted by their despair-
ing conversations on the hopelessness of their love. The
conflict is never resolved; they leave each other, expecting
to continue the affair in the future.

Primarily, Kheifits' contribution to the motion picture
is his success in capturing the Chekhovian atmosphere.
Aleksei Batalov captures the personality of the defeated bu-
reaucrat with perfection, while the yellowish tint of the Yalta
scenes enhances the feeling of boredom and desperation. In
effect, The Lady with the Dog is a peculiarly Russian love
story as well as a social commentary on the hopeless life
of the bourgeoisie in Tsarist Russia.

The pessimistic humanism of the adaptations of Chekhov is matched by the somewhat more optimistic humanism
of Ivan Pyriev's adaptations of Dostoyevsky. Pyriev, who
had formerly specialized in imitations of Aleksandrov's musicals, began filming Dostoyevsky's works with The Idiot in
1958. Although the resulting motion picture was technically
excellent, Pyriev did not diverge one line from the original
work. Nevertheless, The Idiot stands as a milestone in Soviet cinema because it introduced the anti-heroine as the central character of a Russian film. Dostoyevksy's Nastasia
Philippovna could not have been authentically portrayed as a
corrupted, amoral mistress of an equally corrupt aristocrat
under Stalinist socialist realism. Dostoyevsky's hero,

Prince Myshkin, is also too full of flaws to have been made
into a "positive character" under the Zhdanov principles of
"correct" Soviet film-making and literature.

"Little Dramas"

The humanism unleashed during the late 1950's by the
war dramas and the classic adaptations was continued during
the early 1960's in a series of "little dramas" of contemporary life. Dimka (1963), directed by a recent graduate of
the Film Institutes, depicted the plight of a five-year-old boy
in search of a father. After wandering around Moscow,
Dimka selects a young man named Andrei who agrees to take
him to an amusement park. Later, Andrei is brought home
to Dimka's widowed mother. Their meeting is an exercise
in lack of communication but, for Dimka's sake, the young
man promises to return soon. The film is unremarkable except for director Ilya Frezh's attempt to bring the poignant
quality of the literary adaptations into a story of modern Soviet life. As in so many of the Soviet films of contemporary
society, the subject is too frivolous and the situation too un-
realistic to touch the audience's emotions.

Grigori Chukhrai scored a greater success in a contemporary setting with There Was an Old Couple (1965).
Ivan Marin and Vera Kuznetsova brilliantly portray an old
couple who are forced to move in with their daughter Nina
when their own house is burned by fire. They find tragedy
at their new home: Nina has become the mistress of a man
in another town, their son-in-law has become an alcoholic
and their granddaughter is neglected. Quickly, they take
charge of the situation, taking care of the granddaughter and
helping the son-in-law to start a new life. At the climax of
the film, Nina returns and is gently, but firmly told by her
father that her presence in the house could only lead to the
disintegration of the life that her parents have carefully built
for the son-in-law.

Chukhrai's success in There Was an Old Couple lies
in its similarities to the war dramas. It begins with a di-
saster--the loss of the couple's home--and continues with the
broken home, a situation often found in wartime. Chukhrai
was daring enough to admit that women in the contemporary
Soviet Union still run away with lovers and that men in modern Russia can still be depressed enough to become alcoholics
and social outcasts. Soviet audiences were pleased to find a

film in which believable characters faced a tragic situation in
a familiar setting.   Only the constant wisdom and understanding of the old couple occasionally strikes a false note in an
otherwise realistic drama.

The Decline of Soviet Humanism: Political Films

Throughout the years after the de-Stalinization campaign was brought into the open, Soviet writers and film-
makers were frequently reminded that there was a limit to
the degree of creative freedom which the Soviet state would
permit.   As early as the fall of 1957, Khrushchev gave a
garden party for Soviet intellectuals, at which he informed
them that he blamed the Hungarian Revolution of 1956 on a
handful of Hungarian writers who had lost their ideological
orientation.   He then threatened the assembled guests that,
in the event of a similar problem appearing among Soviet
writers and artists, "My hand would not tremble."   The following year, Khrushchev demonstrated the teeth behind the
threat when Boris Pasternak was forced to refuse the Nobel
Prize for Dr. Zhivago.   During the early 1960's, articles in
various provincial journals, a favorite means among the
Kremlin leadership for indirect attack, complained of the
lack of political feeling among film-makers.   In particular,
the articles warned against the "cult of the director."

The greatest blow against non-Socialist humanism in Soviet cinema came in October, 1964, when Nikita Khrushchev
was ousted from the premiership by a coalition of managerial
experts and former associates of Stalin.   As in the years
following the death of Stalin, the impact of the political coup
on the film industry was slow to begin but irresistible.   Before the end of 1965, the effect of the ideological shift towards
Stalinism in the political sphere was reflected in the growing
number of politically-motivated films under production.

Sergei Yutkevich, then 61 years old, contributed Lenin
in Poland (1965) to the campaign to bring ideology back into
Soviet films.   This recent work was, in effect, a return to
the Lenin biographies of Yutkevich's earlier career: The Man
with the Gun (1938) and Three Stories of Lenin (1958).   The
extent of the return can be gauged by the fact that he used
the same actor, Maxim Straukh, to portray Lenin in all three
films.

There is very little action in Lenin in Poland.   Straukh

engages in a series of monologues, criticizing the folly of the
doomed capitalists and Tsarist officials who not only failed to
see the coming Revolution but also imprisoned Lenin.   These
recollections are interrupted by little incidents depicting the
humanity, patience and kindness of Lenin while in exile in
Poland.   Gradually, the audience realizes that the action of
the film takes place before the Revolution.   Hopefully, they
are impressed by Lenin's absolute certainty that the Revolution is coming and that he will be victorious.

Although the film is technically good--Yutkevich was
awarded the prize for Best Direction at the 1966 Cannes Fes-
tival--the subject is dull and the character of Lenin clearly
too perfect.   In his attempt to humanize the founder of the
Soviet Union, Yutkevich failed to delineate any of the personal
flaws that make a character interesting and believable.   The
result is clearly a retreat towards the socialist realist films
which presented Russian audiences with idealized biographies
of their present and former rulers.   It is doubtful that such
works will be useful except as educational films.

A somewhat more original note was undertaken by
Mikhail Romm in his semi-documentary, Ordinary Fascism
(1965).   Romm used montage effects and trick camera work
similar to those employed in a famous sensationalist work of
Italian film journalism, Mondo Cane (1961), to provide a
highly personal view of Nazi Germany.   Its political importance lies in the climax of the film, in which Romm implies
that Germany is headed towards a resurgance of Nazism.   To
accomplish this, the director mixes images of anti-semitic
attacks during the period of Hitler's rise to power with recent photographs of the desecration of a Jewish synagogue in
Munich.   Elsewhere, Romm's narrator notes that cultural decadence and the power of German industrialists paved the
path towards Nazism.   The end of the film depicts scenes of
life in modern West Germany, replete with implied decadence
and industrial growth.   The skillful propaganda allows the
audience to make their own assumptions about the parallels
between the two periods.

The explanation for the contemporary propaganda in
Ordinary Fascism lies in Soviet foreign policy of the post-
war period.   In the mid-1950's, Khrushchev and Malenkov
began to preach peaceful competition with the major Western
powers and the anti-American propaganda campaign was relaxed.   The more vicious of the post-war films about American spies and perfidy were removed from circulation.   In

place of the United States, the Soviet Union chose West Germany as the arch-imperialist. Every action of the West German government--the decision to rearm, the decision to join the Common Market, the growth of German trade relations with Eastern Europe--was attacked as further proof of Germany's return to expansionism and militarism. By 1965, the Soviet Union had to continually remind the Communist states of Eastern Europe that Germany was still dangerous. Ordinary Fascism was clearly an offshoot of the anti-German propaganda campaign. It was removed from general distribution recently when diplomatic recognition of West Germany by the Soviet Union seemed imminent.

Recent Trends in Soviet Cinema

        With the exception of the "little dramas" of contemporary Soviet life, all the genres of Soviet film-making since Stalin's death are still in evidence. Literary adaptations from Chekhov, Dostoyevsky and Tolstoy are still being made, although none has matched the scope of Sergei Bondarchuk's grandiose showpiece, War and Peace (1963-1968). In particular, a 1971 production of Chekhov's Uncle Vanya, directed by the young, highly acclaimed Andrei Mikhalkov-Konchalovsky, is praised by some Western critics as the most authentic interpretation of Chekhov's intentions on or off the legitimate stage. Dramas using a wartime setting are not as common as during the early 1960's, primarily because the Second World War was overused as a setting ten years ago, but an occasional film similar in plot to The Cranes Are Flying is reported in the Soviet press. Musicals whose style recalls the early work of Alexandrov (e. g. , Carnival in Moscow of 1956) are still shown, although Alexandrov himself has turned to the genre of propagandistic biographies (e. g. , Lenin in Switzerland of 1966), apparently in order to set an example for young film-makers not to follow his early career by specializing in "safe" apolitical works.

        Despite the continued existence of the genres, the spirit of innovation has clearly left the Soviet film industry. The literary adaptations of 19th-century classics have become almost desperately faithful to the originals, with the directors reluctant to risk the criticism of "tampering" that was applied to directors who personally interpreted such works during the early 1960's. Creativity still exists, but only in the sense that the directors creatively apply their knowledge of film techniques to bring the ideas of long-dead authors

Fig. 16. Sergei Bondarchuk (with megaphone) directing War and Peace. (Source: Soviet Embassy)

into motion picture form.   Film versions of operas and bal-
lets by Russian composers have reverted back in several
cases (e. g. , <u>Plisetskaya Dances</u> of 1964) to simple film rec-
ords of performances on stage.

The reasons for this reversion to a less humanistic
Soviet cinema lie in the intellectual and political climate of
the Soviet Union.   When film directors began to innovate during Khrushchev's de-Stalinization campaign, they did so in
full knowledge of the existence of the mechanism for censorship.   The various censorship officers did not disappear from
1956 until 1964; they were merely under orders to permit
more material of an apolitical nature to be produced.   In
most cases, the directors who dared to innovate were extremely careful to avoid implied criticisms of life under the
contemporary Soviet leadership, although a handful of motion
pictures including <u>There Was an Old Couple</u> cautiously mentioned such domestic problems as alcoholism.   Mikhalkov-
Konchalovsky's second feature film, <u>Asya Klyachina, Who
Loved But Did Not Marry</u> (1966), was a rare case of a contemporary Soviet drama which overstepped the limits of modern socialist propriety.   The unfortunate young director's
work was banned until he had proven his reliability by directing an adaptation of a 19th-century classic, <u>A Nest of Gentle-
folk</u> (1969).   This punitive action probably influenced other
young directors to avoid the risky genre of "little dramas"
of modern life.   Clearly, Soviet film-makers were not firmly
committed to humanism as a counterbalance to socialist realism.

The political aspect is a reflection of what some writers
called "neo-Stalinism. "   The conservative regime which succeeded Khrushchev in 1964 disapproved of the growing independence of creative workers in the Soviet Union.   In the
view of the collective leadership, the humanistic movement
that had been encouraged by Khrushchev as an indirect attack
on Stalinism was ill-advised in the first place and was now
getting out of control.   The "Prague summer" of 1968 confirmed their fears of the dangers to the stability of socialist
society inherent in de-Stalinization and weak ideological control of intellectuals.   With an eye to the continued survival
of their own regime, the present leaders of the Soviet Union
will undoubtedly continue to limit artistic freedom in the Soviet film industry.   While the absurdities of Zhdanovism will
probably not reappear, the basic principle that cinema is an
organ of propaganda and must be subservient to the political
needs of the State has never been effectively modified in the
Soviet Union, and it is unlikely that it will be changed in the
near future.

CHAPTER 7

CINEMA AS CRITIC:
EASTERN EUROPE, 1955-1971

Despite almost thirty years of Communist control, the cinema is one of the most important of all the arts for the intelligentsia of Eastern Europe. The film directors of Poland, Hungary, Yugoslavia and Czechoslovakia are today considered among the finest in the field. In accordance with the reality of cultural independence, each of the Eastern European states has created its own "school" of film-making. The three eldest of these "schools" are similar in their pre-war traditions and in their interest in depicting the problems of socialist society or offering the alternative values of the past. In effect, the cinema in Eastern Europe has developed into a means of intellectual criticism of the Soviet-inspired status quo.

This was not true during the bleak years immediately after the war. The economic hardships in Eastern Europe all but destroyed the film industries of Czechoslovakia and Hungary, but these were resurrected in the Soviet model. New industries were created in Yugoslavia, Rumania, Bulgaria and, ultimately, Albania, with the aid of Soviet technical and ideological experts. This aid was a mixed blessing, particularly for the three countries with long-established film-making traditions. In the words of Czech film critic A. J. Liehm, "the rigidity of the Stalinist system, the schematicism and vulgarity of Zhdanov 'aesthetics' " was imposed on the film industry. As Stalinism gave way to de-Stalinization in 1955-56, the regimes in Eastern Europe began to give more freedom in making films according to the preferences of the directors. Although controls have been reimposed from time to time in almost all of the countries involved, in general the trend, until recently, has been towards liberalization.

Several administrative factors are involved in the

127

reasons behind the cinema's ability to maintain some of its
creativity and independence in Eastern Europe and the corresponding failure in the Soviet Union. Soviet film-making was
handicapped almost from birth by the "Lenin proportion" described in Chapter 2. Although the Lenin proportion was too
vague to be put into practice, it had the indirect effect of
limiting entertainment films to very frivolous or classical
works. At the same time, it encouraged the Soviet film studios to produce scores of propaganda films whose entertainment value was nil. The studios of Eastern Europe were
never subjected to the "guidance" of the Lenin proportion,
even during the bleakest days of the industry in 1948-55, and
did not have to work under this handicap.

A second factor was the contrast between twenty-five
years of Stalinist socialist ideological control in the U.S.S.R.
and the much briefer period of Stalinism in Eastern Europe.
Unlike Soviet directors, film-makers in Hungary and Czechoslovakia had an opportunity to see American and British films
without ideologically-motivated editing. This gave the directors of Eastern Europe a basis for comparison which the Soviet directors lacked. The personnel purges which were
linked to ideological control in the Soviet Union also occurred
in Eastern Europe, but none of these was as severe as the
original model. At least, none decimated the national studios
as thoroughly as the combined effects of the Soviet purges of
the 30's and late 40's. Many of the Eastern European directors of the pre-war cinema were able to survive the Stalinist
period, continuing their influence as artists and teachers to
the present day.

Eastern Europe, like the Soviet Union, experienced
severe cutbacks in feature production in those nations where
a film industry had been established before the war. Poland,
for example, produced only eighteen features from 1950
through 1955. The reasons for this low output were partly
political but largely economic. The new generation graduat-
ing from the instruction of experienced pre-war directors in
Lodz, Budapest and Prague were encouraged to use their
creative energies on short films. They complied, knowing
that they would eventually be permitted to expand into feature
film-making. This explains the high quality of "shorts" and
comparatively inexpensive animated films produced in Eastern
Europe since the early 1950's. It also accounts, in part,
for the sudden emergence of major young film directors
throughout Eastern Europe in 1960-1961, when budgets allowed for expansion of the local film industries.

Social Criticism in Eastern European Film

A spirit of criticism inherited from de-Stalinization and the relatively successful 1956 revolt in Poland existed in Eastern Europe during the late 1950's. This was the beginning of the end of Stalinist unity in the area and the birth of intellectual reaction against State-directed orthodoxy in both politics and the arts. In film, the older, pre-war directors may have instilled some of their criticisms of the new regimes into their students. It is certain, however, that Eastern European writers and philosophers during the late 1950's were heavily engaged in criticism of the Communist regimes as "dehumanizing." The works of Milovan Djilas were widely read by the intellectuals of the more advanced states--without official permission, of course--and even the neo-Stalinist society of Czechoslovakia bred a strong humanist movement spearheaded by the philosophers Karel Kosik and Ivan Svitak.

In the Soviet Union, these factors were either absent or greatly diminished in influence. By 1955, all of the truly creative directors of the Eisenstein-Pudovkin-Dovzhenko period had been dead for years and repression against "bourgeois humanism" was far more severe. The new Soviet directors were trained in orthodox schools of film-making by the survivors of the Stalin era and, unlike directors in other Eastern European states, had to prove their orthodoxy by being Party members. Censorship was, in general, much tighter and, if the new generation had criticisms of their society, they were not given the opportunity to voice them. This was not true in Poland, Hungary, Czechoslovakia and Yugoslavia.

Not all Eastern European films demonstrate intellectual reaction against the regimes. Those of Bulgaria, for example, seem to be as strictly censored as Soviet films; their most elaborate themes involve nothing more controversial than anti-fascism. Yugoslav feature films tend to be high in entertainment value, increasingly high in technical expertise and as frank in the portrayal of sex and violence as French cinema, but they lack social criticism. Murder of a Switchboard Operator (1967), for example, is a well-executed melodrama of sordid reality climaxed by a grisly murder, but the setting could have been West Germany or France equally as well as Yugoslavia. While this is in itself an important statement about the nature of Yugoslav society--that it is becoming indistinguishable from the bourgeois

societies of the West--the purpose of the film is to entertain,
not to analyze a social problem. <u>The Twelve Chairs</u> (1970),
a screen adaptation of an NEP-period Soviet satire (which has
recently been made into a long, chaotic Russian comedy film),
was primarily an American film, although all of the technicians, locations and extras were Serbian. Even in Poland
and pre-invasion Czechoslovakia, the two centers of "rele-
vant" film-making in Eastern Europe, a majority of the films
produced have been either purely entertainment "froth" or
pro-regime propaganda.

It must also be observed that not all of the problems
of Eastern European society make interesting or marginally
acceptable material for the cinema. The failures of Communist agricultural policy, for example, could conceivably be a
theme for a critical Eastern European film, but no regime in
the area--including Yugoslavia--has become so tolerant that
an artist can freely comment on the subject. Expressions of
local nationalism, however, are almost universal throughout
the area, despite the anti-Russian overtones of some of these
works. The problems of the individual in a heavily structured
society have been occasionally examined by Eastern European
directors, particularly in Czechoslovakia before the 1968 invasion. Perhaps the most daring criticisms of post-war society to be explored by the film-makers of the area have been
of the alienation of the post-war generation. This has been
reflected primarily in Hungarian and Czech works.

Romantic Nationalism: Search for Old Values

The nationalistic celebration of pre-Communist regime
history and literature is a form of intellectual rebellion
against the Eastern European status quo. During the Stalinist
era, such expressions of nationalism were forbidden because
they ran counter to the Russian attempts to pattern Eastern
European culture to the Russian-Soviet model. Later, as the
Soviet cultural bloc in Eastern Europe showed signs of weak-
ness, this form of nationalism became less distasteful to the
local Communist regimes, partly because it is not necessarily
an anti-socialist force. In fact, for the more independent regimes such as Albania and Rumania, romantic nationalism can
be considered a movement that supports the regime in its announced policy of independent (read non-Russian) alignment.
It also serves as a unifying influence in the Balkan multi-
nation states. In its most radical form, however, romantic
nationalism is a search for alternative values in the past to
those of the Communist regime.

Romantic nationalism seems to have first appeared in the works of Czech film-makers, where the largest number of pre-war directors remained active in the industry after the Communist take-over. It found its first expression in screen adaptations of Czech classics and legends, as early as 1947. This trend was first seen in a reaction against the oppressive atmosphere of the early 1950's by three directors: Jiri Trnka, Karel Stekly and Vaclav Krska.

Jiri Trnka's life and work can be considered a symbol of the artist against society. Born in 1912, Trnka was, until the Second World War, the director of a well-known puppet theater in Bohemia, where puppetry remains an accomplished art form. In 1945, he became one of the directors of the Prague Puppet and Cartoon Studio, a position which he held until 1954. In that year, Trnka followed the direction of the first post-1948 film anthology of Czech folk tales with a new film version of The Good Soldier Schweik.

The story of Schweik has unique significance in the context of Stalinist Czechoslovakia. As H. Gordon Skilling, the Canadian authority on Czech culture, has observed, Schweik's creative gold-bricking is directly opposed to the patriotic industrial self-sacrifice desired by the Stalinist state. A society which demands complete respect and obedience to its institutions cannot accept the sneering, anti-establishment Schweik as a national hero.

Perhaps the authorities found the strongly anti-authoritarianism of Trnka's Schweik objectionable; more likely, Jiri Trnka's other "traditional" values were equally outspoken and at odds with the doctrines of socialist realism. Whatever the cause, his subsequent "retirement" lasted nine years, one of the few cases of probable reprisal against a nationalist artist in Eastern Europe.

Less than a year after the completion of Trnka's Schweik, Karel Stekly began to participate in the romantic nationalist movement. Stekly, nine years Trnka's senior, was a minor pre-war director who spent the years 1948-1955 creating pro-regime propaganda films such as Anna the Proletarian (1952). In 1955, he directed a live-actor version of a Czech folk tale, The Piper of Strakonice, the subject of a 1932 Czech film. Two years later, Stekly completed a two-part version of The Good Soldier Schweik. As a result of the inconsistent policy of neo-Stalinism, softened by early de-Stalinization in 1956, Stekly was permitted to continue

directing screen versions of Czech literary works until his
retirement from active film-making in 1963.

The early work of Vaclav Krska--The Revolutionary
Year 1848, Mikolas Ales, etc.--and Otakar Vavra's 1957 trilogy on the life of Jan Hus represent most of the Czech involvement in the non-literary side of romantic nationalism.
A national history the most celebrated event of which is a
17th-century military disaster is not easily applied to historical romances. Slovak directors, however, have been active
in the task of glorifying Slovak national history, particularly
the lives of noted Slovak highwaymen. These, of course,
have been transformed by Martin Frić and other directors
into Slavic Robin Hoods and proto-revolutionaries. Other nations have also developed this form of expression, including
the Rumanians, the Poles, the Hungarians and, in their one
major feature, the Albanians.

Of Albanian cinema in general, suffice it to say that
it provides work for some 200 Albanians--not enough to staff
a single large studio in the United States--and that only the
1953 epic, Great Warrior Skenderbeg, has been released in
the West. Since it stars a Georgian actor in the title role
and was filmed by a Soviet director, the Albanian claim that
this was the first Albanian feature is not very secure. Great
Warrior Skenderbeg set a pattern in the small world of Albanian film-making: at least one of the two or three features
made each year in Tirana is based on a historical theme.
As expected, the Skenderbeg episode is one of the most popular subjects, rivaled only by the anti-fascist resistance of
thirty years ago.

The Rumanian film industry, like that of Albania, is
a post-war phenomenon. Topical films are still rare, although they are reportedly gaining influence and prestige. In
general, the large budgets and modern film equipment have
been lavished on a series of grand historical spectacles,
suitable for foreign export. These began with Tudor, a film
depicting the swashbuckling exploits of a 19th-century revolutionary, Tudor Vladmirescue, filmed in 1964 by Lucian Bratu.
Tudor has been followed by a large output of historical adventures, occasionally aided by French co-production (e. g., The
Immortals, released in 1966) but recently entirely Rumanian
in production and financing (e. g., Rape of the Maidens and
Return of the Outlaws, both directed by Dinu-Constantin Cocea
in 1968).

Not all Rumanian films view the past in a rosy light.
Mircea Muresan's Flaming Winter (1966), based on the novel
The Uprising, is similar to many motion pictures set in the
pre-revolutionary era.   The socialist film industry of Bucha-
rest invariably depicts the late 19th century and early 20th
as a time of brutality and deception, when Rumanian artists
suffered because of government indifference and the Rumanian
peasants suffered under a feudal system.   Flaming Winter depicts the landed class as decadent and the bourgeois hero
Baloleanu as weak and basically conservative.   The climactic
revolt of the peasants is realistically filmed in all its leader-
less violence.   Through this style of consistently describing
the pre-revolutionary period as tragic and violent, the Rumanian film industry attempts to condemn the nationalism of
the old regime while maintaining its praise of ancient Rumanian nationalism in the historical spectacles.

Both the Albanian and Rumanian works can be considered reactions against modern realities only in the sense
that they permit the artist and his audience to escape into a
near-mythical heroic period.   They tend to emphasize the
miraculous personal abilities of the hero, but their atmosphere of unreality is so pronounced that it would be false to
declare this a return to the cult of the individual--a Stalinist
principle--except in the mildest form.   As mentioned earlier,
the glorification of national history serves the two regimes'
desire for popular support of their extremely nationalist, de-
fiantly independent foreign policies.   Film-makers in both
countries are careful to use those periods in history--such
as the Turkish wars--in which the entire population acted as
one.   In this context, the celebration of all-Albanian defense
and all-Rumanian struggle have a unifying propaganda effect.
In addition, the films in question are a means to get hard
currency through export (and also a means of producing a desirable State-owned commodity on which the Rumanians can
spend their wages instead of on imported consumer goods).

The Quest For Polish Chivalry

Jan Szczepanski notes in Polish Society that the syn-
thesis of traditional and modern personality traits has produced a hybrid Polish personality ideal that still includes a
readiness to defend the Fatherland, self-sacrifice for a lost
cause and self-discipline.   These traits are particularly vis-
ible in the intelligentsia which, according to Szczepanski,
formerly copied the ideals of the Polish military aristocracy.

In Polish cinema, evidence supporting Szczepanski's statement can be found in the romanticism of Aleksandr Ford, Jerzy Hoffman and Andrzej Wajda.

Aleksandr Ford is the dean of Polish film-making and was one of its chief administrators until the 1970's. This was probably due, in large part, to his flight to the Soviet Union in 1939 and his subsequent work in Soviet films during the German occupation. Since the end of the war, he has continually found inspiration in subjects from classical Polish history, beginning with his post-war feature, The Youth of Chopin (1952), and culminating in the grand spectacle, Knights of the Teutonic Order (1960). The latter is similar in many ways to Sergei Eisenstein's Alexander Nevsky, with the logical exceptions that the technical quality of the 1960 film is far superior and the villainous invading army is German rather than Livonian. The heroic defenders are Polish nobles, depicted as far more aristocratic than the defenders of Novgorod in the Eisenstein film. No longer an unusually innovative director, Ford succeeded in surviving the socialist realist period of the early 1950's and has been able to bring a certain degree of technical elegance to the glorification of old Poland.

Jerzy Hoffman is one of the younger directors who have been influenced by Ford and his contemporaries. Although he is best known for his documentaries, in 1969 he completed Colonel Wolodyjowski, a historical spectacle similar in many ways to Knights of the Teutonic Order. Apart from technical superiority to the earlier film--Wolodyjowski had the largest budget of any Polish film up to that time-- there was a greater interest in the personalities of the two leading characters: the aristocratic Polish hero and the almost revolutionary Ukrainian villain. The choice of the theme of the chivalrous noble defeating the forces of change is interesting and can be analyzed as a sentimental longing for the old Poland which Hoffman, born in 1932, never really experienced.

Superior in artistry to both Ford and Hoffman is the work of the prolific Andrzej Wajda, perhaps the most famous of the new generation of Polish directors. Wajda has exhibited a strong interest in the Polish ideal of self-sacrifice in many of his works; he displays a fascination with its aristocratic roots and its value in the modern era. His first feature, A Generation, filmed towards the end of the exclusively socialist realist period of Polish cinema in 1954, is a

transitional work between Zarkhi formula writing and the later
creativity. The five protagonists of <u>A Generation</u> are youthful members of the resistance, but their reasons for joining
are not ideologically pure. At the end of the film, all but
one of the group have moved closer to the ideal of the positive hero (the one exception being a particularly weak character who has committed suicide), but they do so for very personal reasons.

Andrzej Wajda's second feature film also centers on
the question of Polish heroism during the Second World War.
<u>Kanal</u>, however, is more explicit in both setting and theme.
Its story begins as the remnants of the Polish forces involved
in the Warsaw resistance of 1944 are being driven underground by the German forces. The Soviet Army, whose in-
action the Poles often blamed for the defeat of the uprising,
is dimly seen encamped on the wrong side of the Vistula to
help the defenders of Warsaw. The film follows the plight
of a Polish platoon trapped in the sewers of the city. The
atmosphere throughout <u>Kanal</u> is gloomy: the characters know
that they are doomed and only the courage and determination
of an aloof, aristocratic officer can save them.

The end of the film is typical of Wajda. After under-
going terrible hardships to find escape for his men, the Polish captain discovers that the cowardice of his lieutenant has
defeated his purpose. The commander calmly murders the
betrayer of the platoon as soon as the two officers leave the
underground death-trap, then turns his back on freedom to
look for his lost command. The audience understands that
the commander will probably be unable to find the platoon
and that, if he does, it is now impossible that they will escape. His action is the ultimate in aristocratic self-sacrifice.

In <u>Kanal</u>, Wajda's attitude towards the old ideals is
ambiguous. On the one hand, it is clear that he views the
self-sacrifice of the commander as futile and somehow out
of touch with reality. The inevitable doom of the officer can
be interpreted as symbolic of the inevitable doom of the class
which he represents. It is known from subsequent Polish
history that the Warsaw uprising was, in fact, the final gesture of the old Poland against the revolutionary forces of the
Twentieth Century. On the other hand, the sympathetic treatment of the officer and the use of his sacrifice as the climax
of the film indicate that Wajda sees the grand gestures of the
vanished class as a value not wholly lacking in merit.

Figs. 17 & 18.   Scenes from Kanal, an early nationalistic
work by Wajda.   (Source: Film Polski)

Fig. 19. Climactic murder of the cowardly lieutenant in <u>Kanal</u>. (Source: Film Polski)

Apparently the Polish audience agreed with him; Kanal was one of the most popular features in Poland at the time of its release in 1956. It is tempting to relate its theme and its popularity as a kind of catalyst to the nationalistic outbreaks in Poland of that year; it is far more likely that, rather than creating them, Kanal voiced sentiments already held by the Polish people.

Wajda has been subject to official criticism and censorship for his lack of attention to socialist realism and the "needs" of the state. By 1959, however, his popularity abroad influenced the film administrators to grant him larger budgets, such as the one granted for Lotna (1959). Lotna was one of the first Polish films to express the lyricism of the "new wave" cinema of the 1960's, but its theme was essentially the same as Kanal's. Again, in its story of a Polish horse cavalry unit in 1939, there is the ambiguous attitude towards the grand, futile gestures of the old Polish personality ideal. The magnificent scene of the cavalry charge against the invading Nazi army is, without question, the most blatant celebration of a glorious nationalistic anachronism.

Jancso of Hungary

Much of the output of Hungarian studios has been devoted to historical spectacles, including Last of the Nabobs. Most of these are probably influenced by the Rumanian epics; at least one Rumanian epic director has been active in the Hunnia Studios of Budapest.

One Hungarian director stands out, however, as being both innovative and controversial in working with subjects out of Hungarian and Soviet history. All of the work of Miklos Jancso is said to reflect his studies in art history at the University of Budapest and his almost obsessive fascination with violence. From newsreels, Jancso turned to feature film-making at the beginning of the Hungarian "thaw" in the early 1960's. He first received attention abroad for My Way Home (1964), in which he used the setting of the Eastern front during the Second World War, a popular "approved" setting for Eastern European films. It begins as a simple story of the growing friendship between a Hungarian prisoner and his young Russian guard. This theme is developed in a pastoral setting until, toward the end, the Russian is killed and Red Army partisans appear to "capture" the prisoner, beat and humiliate him and, perhaps, kill him. It is one of the most anti-Soviet scenes in any film from the region and, for this reason, Jancso can be loosely grouped with other romantic nationalist directors. My Way Home can be considered a denial of the possibility for brotherhood between the Soviet Russians and those who do not share their system.

Later films by Jancso have also been set in historical settings, although rarely as recent as that in My Way Home. The Red and the White also relates the progressively tragic experiences of a Hungarian trying to live in the Soviet Union. The protagonist of The Red and the White (1967) which is set during the Russian Civil War, is an active volunteer for the Soviet cause. Most of the film is an unrelieved indictment of the inhuman brutality of the Whites--the anti-Communist Russian forces--but the ending is a similar act of cruelty by the Reds, in which the film's heroine is executed "by mistake." Far removed from the positive-looking principles of socialist realist drama, Jancso hints that the Reds were, perhaps, no better than their ideological enemies.

Between these two films, Jancso completed The Herding (1965), an almost documentary account of the aftermath of the Hungarian Revolution of 1848. There is little plot and no central character; Jancso simply details the methods by which the victorious counter-revolutionaries tortured and tricked confessions and betrayals from their prisoners. The analogy to more recent times is, perhaps, just subtle enough to avoid official censorship. Official interpretations describe the work as anti-nationalist because the persecutors are Hungarian reactionaries. Nevertheless, it implies that, while the past was full of violence and political terror, Stalinism is no better. It denies the progress of the human condition promised by Marxism. In the pessimism of this and other works, Jancso is a critic of his times.

In summary, celluloid romantic nationalism fulfills different purposes in each of the states of Eastern Europe. In Albania, it has been used to encourage the growth of all-Albanian nationalism in counteraction to centuries of divided culture and experience among the people of the country. In Rumania, it is a form of escape from the socialist reality. In Czechoslovakia and, decidedly, in Poland, it is an expression of national pride and of the very different traditional values of the two countries. In Hungary, Miklos Jancso has used historical settings to imply that the new order of socialism is not fundamentally different from the violence-filled old order. In all of these instances, with the possible

exception of Albania, romantic nationalism is a demonstration
of dissatisfaction with the way things are. In the West, such
criticism is common and the examples described above would
appear very mild. For Eastern Europe, however, this
amount of criticism is a radical departure from the Stalinist
period of the arts.

The Alienation of Youth in East European Films

It is the official policy of the governments of Eastern
Europe to deny that the youth of their countries are alienated
or apathetic or subject to any of the confusion which is common among the youth of capitalist countries. Despite the authorized picture of Eastern European youth as dedicated
builders of a socialist future, screenplay authors and film
directors of the region have attempted to discuss the very
real "youth problem." At first limited to propagandistic
statements against local "hooliganism," the cinema of Eastern
Europe became more thoughtful by the early 1960's. Although
often critical of the post-war generation, film-makers have
continued to progress in portraying the realistic reactions of
the socialist generation to the social system into which they
were born.

The realistic portrayal in film of the problems of
youth may have begun in Hungary, in 1955, with a film by
the veteran actor-director Zoltan Fabri, a graduate of the
Horthy era Academy of Dramatic Arts. Merry-Go-Round
(1955) was his third feature. Like many of his films, it is
set in rural Hungary.

The plot of Merry-Go-Round is a somewhat socialistic
version of Romeo and Juliet. The daughter of an independent
farmer meets a young member of a farmer's cooperative at
a county fair and, in a remarkably lyrical sequence, the two
fall in love. When the peasant comes to the girl's father to
ask for her hand, he refuses, intending to marry the girl off
to another independent farmer. The young lovers are forced
to meet in secret; in the meantime, it is revealed that the
cooperative is on the verge of bankruptcy and the independent
farmer's aid is all that can save the region from economic
disaster. Fortunately for almost everyone, the father finally
relents after much soul-searching and introspection, and both
permits the two lovers to wed and joins the cooperative. The
future looks brighter for both the radical peasants and the
newlyweds.

Above all, <u>Merry-Go-Round</u> is a pleasant, unusually well-executed story of peasant love. Despite its lyrical atmosphere, however, <u>Merry-Go-Round</u> touches on many of the problems facing rural youth in Eastern Europe. The young lovers are found to be both respectful and at odds with the traditional values of the older generation of peasants; at the same time, there is a clear hint that the economically unsuccessful cooperative may not be a viable alternative. Fabri gave special attention to the character of the father, who seems, at times, almost to become a tragic hero caught between his personal morality and the forces of change. The one constant in the film is the love between the two young people, an unusually individualistic theme for early post-war Hungarian film.

The years following the Hungarian Revolt of 1956 were not fruitful years for social criticism. Although feature film production remained high in quantity--except, unaccountably, in 1958--the content and quality of the new films reflected increased censorship and ideological control. It also reflected the apparent tendency of film-goers to prefer frivolous entertainment pictures during hard times, a tendency which was apparent in American films during the Depression and in German films during the Second World War. No films on a subject as controversial as the youth problem appeared again until the 1960's.

During the early years of the last decade, several films involved the problems of youth, but these tended to be comedies rather than serious works. Underlying the humor, however, there was occasional concealed criticism and comment on Hungarian society. In Istvan Szabo's <u>Father</u> (1966), for example, a young man hides from reality behind the fantasies he creates about his long-dead father. In his daydreams, he pictures his father as a partisan leader--an acceptable hero, of course. He also conjures up the image of his father as a political leader of the Horthy period--an unacceptable hero by the standards of the regime which, nevertheless, remains impressive to the young man's friends. In all of the fantasies, the father is free of the drab aura of modern Hungarian life; thus, he becomes a romantic figure.

It would be unfair to state that all Hungarian cinema during the early 1960's took a satiric interest in youth. In <u>The Age of Daydreaming</u> (1964), Istvan Szabo reportedly created a touching and sympathetic portrait of the development of a young man. In this early work, his view of the

problems of youth is highly personalized, but the problems
which are most thoroughly developed in the film are emotional and sentimental, not social. The hero, although still
a young man, is already a television engineer; his role in
the society is established. Szabo can thus concentrate on the
young man's search for emotional fulfillment.

For the examination of the political and social problems of the younger generation, Hungarian cinema had to
wait until 1969, when the nonconformist Miklos Jancso turned
his attention toward youth in The Confrontation. For this
work, Jancso again evaded official condemnation by using a
historical setting: the late 1940's. As in his earlier films,
Jancso incorporates much of the newsreel style into the narrative of young Communist students trying to organize a non-
religious college. Alistair Whyte, a British critic, describes
the film as "almost a musical," with the crusading students
interrupting their work frequently to dance and sing. This
may well be a throwback to the halcyon days of the Hungarian
movie musicals. The gaiety, however, is only a mask for
the confrontation of the title between a reformist leader who
wishes to win over the Catholic opposition by example and a
second leader who insists on the necessity of force. In the
end, the resulting power struggle brings police intervention
and an end to the experiment, but the more ruthless leader
is also clearly the victor. The mood of the film throughout
is ominous and the outcome of the struggle is a further reflection of Jancso's pessimism.

The idea of the younger generation being eager to
create change but opposed to the Communist intimidating
methods to force change is continued in The Falcons (1970),
directed by Istvan Gaal, one of the youngest feature directors
in Hungary. In The Falcons the theme of youth in opposition
to an authoritarian established order is carried out symbolically within the context of a "scientific" institution for the
training of hunting birds. The description of the trained falcons as "the police of the air," the institution's lengthy code
of rules for the care of the birds and the conduct of the personnel, and the authoritarian personality of the head trainer
all point towards social commentary. The youthful protagonist, a newcomer to the research station, becomes progressively fearful and resentful of the atmosphere of the institution until, at the end of the film, he sets off alone across
the barren plain surrounding the station, determined to leave.

The analogies and symbols used in The Falcons are

not subtle. They allow Gaal to film some spectacular scenes of the birds gliding through the air above the steppes, seizing their prey, etc. It is an example of precisely what Soviet film has lost: the ability to make a socially significant comment while remaining artistically creative. It may also be a sign that the ideological control of Hungarian film-making is weakening. Allegory may become the means of escape from the danger of discussing Hungarian youth in either satiric or strongly personal terms.

Cinema in Czechoslovakia has been orientated for a long time toward the examination of society through the analysis of the daily lives of ordinary people. Czech culture has a strong emphasis on humanism running counter to the "scientific" spirit of socialism. The programs of the Czech reformers in 1968 reflected the desire to humanize their society; the Czech directors' fascination with depiction of ordinary people facing unheroic situations stems from the same humanist values. Czech directors gave rise to a school of realistic cinema, both serious as in The Shop on the High Street (1965) and comic as in Firemen's Ball, rivaling the work of any other national cinema.

Among the foremost of these directors is Milos Forman, the director of Firemen's Ball and an early graduate of the post-war Prague Film School. Forman's first two features, Peter and Pavla (1963) and A Blonde in Love (1965), deal with individuals trying to escape the drabness of their lives through love affairs, either real or imagined. In Peter and Pavla, Forman traces the efforts of an inept young store detective to attach himself romantically to an indifferent older girl. In the second feature, a young factory worker becomes infatuated with a pianist in a dance band and fantasizes that their one-night affair is the beginning of a serious romance. The blonde's efforts to continue the affair place her in conflict with the musician and society. In both films, Forman has succeeded in combining satire with sympathy for the plight of young people looking for romance in an unromantic society. In addition, in both films Forman touches briefly on the small irritations of socialist life, such as a young worker's difficulties in finding enough money to marry with. Later films by other Czech directors, Jan Nemec's Martyrs of Love (1966) for example, reflect similar themes and similar attitudes.

Jiri Menzel's "Closely Watched Trains"

     Jiri Menzel is one of the youngest of the well-known
Czech directors. His first full-length feature, Closely
Watched Trains, is an adaptation of a short novel by the
popular Czech author Bohumil Hrabal, who collaborated with
Menzel on the screenplay for the film. Menzel was 27 years
old when he completed Closely Watched Trains; he was only
29 when it became the first Czech film to win the Oscar for
Best Foreign Film in 1968.

     Closely Watched Trains is, in one sense, a sophisti-
cated sex comedy. Set in a small town near Prague during
the German occupation, it can be described as the adventures
of a young man in search of an end to his virginity. In the
course of this odyssey, the young man--Milos Hrma--has all
kinds of misunderstandings with the older generation and frequent clashes with various officials.

     In a prologue to the action of the film, Hrma under-
scores the rifts between the generations by describing his
own family's reactions to the German occupation. His grand-
father, a patriotic circus magician, is killed when he hero-
ically tries to prevent the German tanks from entering Prague
by hypnotizing the enemy tank drivers. Hrma's father, on
the other hand, has ignored the occupation and continues to
collect a pension awarded to him through an error by his
railroad union. Hrma himself is pleased with the uniform
supplied to him by the Germans as a station guard--a position assigned him by an all-pervasive bureaucracy--but is indifferent to the repetitive exhortations and propaganda voiced
by his distant superiors.

     During the first half of the film, the audience is intro-
duced to a representative of these superiors--Zednicek, the
quisling official. Zednicek first appears at the station (his
entry "is reminiscent of Lohengrin on the swan or Field-
Marshal Keitel entering the captured cities ... ") to explain
"the situation of our armies fighting for the freedom of the
people of Europe, whether they appreciate it or not...."
The railroad station staff, particularly the three younger members, ignore the lecture, but Hrma shows a grudging curios-
ity. The official responds gleefully to Hrma's questions by
explaining the situation in detail, then retreats to explanation
by slogan: "When the final battle is being fought, never mind
about your clothes; finery comes after the battle is won."
Finally exasperated by Hrma's repeated "Why?", Zednicek

angrily snaps, "Because it is the Fuehrer's wish and that is enough!"

What Menzel has accomplished in this and similar scenes throughout the film is to comment on contemporary Czech society by disguising the contemporary aspects. For example, to illustrate the concept of "ideological fatigue"-- the rejection of constant propagandistic harangues by the so-cialist population--Menzel transforms the Marxist propagan-dists into the quisling Zednicek. To criticize the drabness and austerity of modern Czechoslovakia, he has disguised the present conditions with images of wartime shortages and con-trols. Perhaps the alien presence in Czech society--the Rus-sian influence--is represented in the film by the despised Wehrmacht soldiers. This technique of hiding his criticisms gives Menzel great freedom to examine the various societal reactions to the young railroad guard's very human, very personal problem.

Disgusted with his inability to prove his manhood, Hrma decides to take his own life. The unsuccessful attempt brings him to the disapproving attention of railroad officials, who announce that he is suspect because of his family's anti-regime record and who threaten him with the charge of "self-mutilation in order to avoid the duties of service for the pro-tection of the Reich." The station-manager blames Hrma's act on the selfishness of the younger generation and the de-cline of morality, complaining that Hrma has jeopardized his promotion to railroad inspector. The Church offers Hrma psychoanalysis. In the end, Hrma's search for sexual ful-fillment leads him to join the partisans and to his subsequent death while destroying a German train. Some critics add that this ending is a challenge to the accepted stereotypes of the resistance, but these critics are too often the same ones who are blind to the deeper significance of the film as social commentary on modern Czechoslovakia.

In Closely Watched Trains, more than in any other Czech film, the director has emphasized the theme that a society without human values has little interest to youth. Hrma is interested in his personal problem and wants the others around him to be sympathetic. Ideology is confusing to him and boring to the other young railroad workers, and the traditional values of patriotism, piety and respect for the nobility--all of which are frequently expressed by the station-manager--mean little or nothing to him. By concentrating on these aspects, Closely Watched Trains appears as a strong,

thoughtful commentary on the problem of alienation among the
young people in modern Eastern Europe.

Youth in Polish Film

        The Polish directors have been less frivolous in their
attitude toward youth in film than either the Czechs or the
Hungarians. They have not indulged as much in satiric comedies on the "youth problem." This may be a holdover from
the earliest post-war films on Polish youth, such as Ford's
Five Boys from Barska Street (1953), which took the view
that all Polish youth needed in order to integrate into Polish
society was re-education, tempered with the threat of punishment. More recent films, such as Wajda's Innocent Sorcerers
(1960), have claimed that some members of the younger generation are not capable of adjustment to society, portraying
them as selfish, purposeless delinquents.

        Wajda's attitude toward youth seems to have softened
during the early 1960's. In 1962, he directed an episode in
a trilogy entitled Love at Twenty. In his segment, a young
girl becomes romantically involved with an older man, played
by the late very popular Polish actor Zbigniev Cybulski. The
two lovers in the film share understanding until they are
joined by the girl's equally young friends. Misunderstanding
and resentment gradually grow between them and the war veteran, and finally the older man, now drunk, is being ridiculed
by the young people. Only at the end of the segment is there
hope that the two lovers can again bridge the generation gap
and move toward reconciliation. Wajda's latest film, Hunting
Flies (1969), also emphasizes the cynicism of the sophisticated
youth of Warsaw as contrasted with the sympathetic character
of a young romantic.

        A great deal has been written by critics about the only
feature by the director Roman Polanski to be made in Poland,
Knife on the Water. This highly experimental film depicts
the interpersonal conflicts among three characters, but particularly between an older and a younger man. I have been
assured by Polish friends that only someone who has perfect
fluency in Polish can appreciate the film fully, because its
dialogue--and the film is mostly dialogue with very little ac-
tion--is idiomatic in the extreme. Knife on the Water shares
a distinction with Wajda's work; it was singled out for special attacks in 1964 by no less an official than First Secretary
Wladyslaw Gomulka.

Jerzy Skolminowski, a director of Polanski's generation, takes a much less critical, more considered view of
youth in his "Andrzej Leszczyc" series of films. Although
his films are flawed by his inexperience and his insistence
on playing the role of the hero himself, Skolminowski has
tried to depict the youth of Poland as aimlessly searching
rather than living selfishly. In the first film of the series,
Ryopsis (1964), the hero is on the verge of military service,
but his mind is elsewhere. Leszczyc dreams of traveling
somewhere, anywhere. Later episodes of the Leszczyc
series place Skolminowski's hero in conflict with draft boards,
with government officials and with the factory environment.

In a later film, Barrier (1966), Skolminowski expanded
his theme by trying to incorporate all the various "barriers"
that divide Polish society, stressing particularly the division
between the pre-war and post-war generations. Unfortunately,
he again relied too little on the visual effects that give motion pictures their greatest potential impact; in other words,
he talked the various topics to death.

It is clear that the youth problem is a very touchy
topic that must be handled with discretion by the directors of
Eastern Europe if they wish to avoid the weight of official
condemnation. Skolminowski recently failed to do this: in
1970, he completed a film entitled Hands Up that has been
completely banned by the Polish authorities. In Poland, evidently, the authorities still demand lip service to the theory
that the difficulties experienced by the younger Polish generation are the fault of the young people themselves, not of society. In Czechoslovakia and Hungary, directors have side-
stepped the problem by adopting a more or less frivolous attitude toward the alienation of the younger generation. Social
comment on the youth problem in these two countries has been
disguised in non-contemporary settings, as in Closely Watched
Trains and The Confrontation, or in allegory and symbolism
as in The Falcons. These subterfuges may continue to be the
only means for expressing guarded criticism of the societies'
failure to respond to the needs of the younger generation for
more education, more housing, better jobs and a humanist attitude. Nevertheless, it must be recognized that the fall of
Gomulka and the growing recognition of dissatisfaction among
Polish youth presage the end of the era when young people in
Eastern European films were depicted as either young Communists or juvenile delinquents.

The Individual in the Films of Eastern Europe

The conflict between the individual and society has
been a favorite theme of writers and philosophers in Eastern
and Central Europe for generations. The great Central European writers of the early twentieth century--Mann, Kafka,
Durrenmatt, Nietzsche--were very concerned with the role of
the artistic individual in an increasingly materialistic, bureaucratic society. The coming of Marxism to ideological power,
with its emphasis on the roles of worker, peasant and Party,
placed a temporary silence on the subject, at least in published and produced works. This situation changed abruptly
in 1956.

Vladimir Kusin maintains that the catalyst for this
change was the 20th Party Congress of the CPSU; he also
implies that the younger generation began to suffer at this
point from "ideological fatigue." The combined effects of
Khrushchev's denunciation of Stalin and almost a decade of
overdone Stalinist propaganda apparently resulted in an awak-
ening interest in non-Party concerns. Whatever the cause,
the year 1956 witnessed a sudden outpouring of concern in
the works of Eastern European artists and intellectuals for
their roles as individuals within the socialist commonwealth.
This was reflected in two feature films released that year,
one in Poland and one in Hungary.

Andrzej Munk was an early graduate of the post-war
Lodz film school who would undoubtedly be better known today
if he had lived during the 1960's. Unfortunately, after completing only three feature films, the talented director was
killed in an automobile crash in 1961, at the age of 38. He
is best known for his first feature, Man on the Track, one
of the two 1956 films that first questioned the role of the
non-conformist individual in socialist society.

Munk used a documentary-style approach to introduce
the hero of his film, Orzechowski, a railroad engineer. The
events leading up to Orzechowski's fatal accident would have
made a suitable subject for a socialist realist film, but Munk
deliberately rejected this opportunity by giving the doomed engineer a uniquely individualistic personality. In effect, Munk
created an evil-tempered, conservative prima donna of a tech-
nician, perfectly competent and self-assured and intolerant of
his "inferiors," the coal stokers. Orzechowski's death is,
in several ways, comparable to the death of one of Wajda's
tragic Polish officers. Both are opposed to the materialism

of the socialist order, both are unbearably proud of their
abilities and occupations, and both are doomed to die serving
the traditional Polish ideal of self-sacrifice. Munk's statement is that the values of at least one skilled worker are
those of the individualist, not of the socialist brotherhood of
laborers, and that these still relate to the ideals of the old,
pre-war society.

Professor Hannibal is a 1956 feature by Zoltan Fabri,
the director of the previous year's successful Merry-Go-
Round. This film, like Man on the Track, is not about the
artist per se, but it is concerned with a conflict between the
individual and the state-oriented society. Its hero is the opposite of the aggressive, anti-social Orzechowski: a weak,
uncertain, sheltered intellectual. The professor of the title
is a historian who writes a scholarly work on the Carthaginian
general Hannibal and finds himself under attack by the state
and his colleagues for composing anti-regime propaganda. As
his society--that of pre-war Hungary, for appearance's sake--
levels more and more pressure against him, the historian attempts to rise to the occasion. At the end of the film, he
is seen symbolically isolated in a barren plaza, looking up-
ward at the camera with a mixed expression of defiance and
confusion. Suddenly, an angry mob descends upon him from
all directions and the terrified scholar "recants" his "error"
by spewing forth some incoherent nonsense about Hannibal
sanctifying the soil of Hungary. The crowd roars its approval of the recantation and his life is spared.

The theme of Professor Hannibal is very clear from
the plot. In an intensely ideological state, the work of the
artist and the scholar is without value unless it serves the
needs of the state. The intrinsic merit of the historian's
story passed unnoticed in the midst of the furor over its supposed ideological content. On the other hand, the nonsense
of the professor's confession saves him and earns the approval of the state. The subterfuge of placing the action in
the Horthy era does not conceal the director's intention to
criticize the position to which artists had been relegated in
Stalinist Hungary.

The failure of the popular revolutions in Eastern Europe in 1956 and the return to stringent ideological controls
forced underground any intellectual discussion of the role of
the creative individual in socialist societies. Renewed discussion of the problem did not re-emerge until the middle
1960's, when it appeared in the films of the "new wave"

Fig. 20. Fabri's Professor Hannibal in the good graces of authority. (Source: Hungarofilm)

Fig. 21. Professor Hannibal attacked by the mob. (Source: Hungarofilm)

Czech directors.   One of the earliest comments on the artist
in a state-oriented society, however, came from a very "old
wave" director who had recently returned from creative exile:
Jiri Trnka, the former puppeteer.

"The Hand" of Jiri Trnka

After his "retirement" ended in 1960, Jiri Trnka returned to work with a filmed marionette version of Midsummer
Night's Dream.   From then until 1965, he averaged one puppet feature film each year, including such intriguing works as
Obsession (1961) and Cybernetic Grandma (1962), both of which
were seen as comments on modern Czech society.

In 1965, Trnka directed his last film, a clear statement of his views on the artist in an oppressive society.
The Hand was only two actors: a tiny puppet and a much
larger human hand.   The puppet represents the artist and is
dressed as an old-fashioned rustic craftsman, engrossed in
making little clay pots.   The hand bursts into his workshop
and, through pantomine, demands that the artist fashion a
clay likeness of itself in a heroic pose.   The artist refuses
and the hand wrecks the shop.   As soon as the puppet can
repair the damage, the hand reappears, now with a touch of
gold braid on its sleeve, and again makes the demand.   The
artist is intimidated into beginning the project, but the work
goes too slowly for the egomaniacal hand.   The artist is then
visited by a flirtatious "lady" hand and has a brief moment
of pleasure dancing, only to find himself caged and a marionette with strings, where before he was an "independent" hand
puppet.

At the end of the film, the puppet-artist is made to
look sick and aged.   The statue is completed, but the artist
"dies" from the effort.   The oppressive hand, now wearing a
glove and a great amount of gold braid, carefully places the
artist on a tiny coffin and covers him with an elaborate medal,
posthumously commemorating his unwilling patriotic service.

No other medium could have stated Trnka's anti-author-
itarian theme so well as the combination of film and puppetry
that he had developed for twenty years.   The result was a
deeply moving short film ... and, evidently, the exasperation
of the authorities with Trnka's politics.   Ill health prevented
him from working during the bright days of the Dubcek
"Prague Summer."   He has made no film since The Hand

and, in his sixties, his further return to film-making in Russian-occupied Czechoslovakia is not likely.

The Individual in Later Czech Films

Evald Schorm, the so-called "conscience" of cinema in Prague, completed his first feature in 1964 and immediately ran into difficulties with the authorities. His Courage for Every Day, whose main character is a Stalinist intellectual who is reluctant to change his beliefs during the Khrushchev de-Stalinization campaign, was banned for over a year. Schorm, of course, is not a Stalinist; he mistakenly believed that by attacking the persecution of the intellectual from an unconventional point of view, he would avoid criticism from ideological conservatives--secret Stalinists--within the Party.

Later films by Schorm have also concentrated on the theme of the unconventional individual pitted against socialist society. In House of Joy, his analysis was whimsical in the story of a primitive folk painter annoyed, bewildered and stubbornly unresponsive to the attempts of two officials to register him for life insurance. Pastor's End (1968) struck a farcical note with its con artist protagonist posing as a cleric pitted against a Communist schoolteacher in a small village. The film ends with the "priest" falling too far into the role and becoming entrapped by Church dogma, making him vulnerable to the state-supported attacks of the teacher. Forced to reveal himself as a fraud, the "hero" finds himself deserted by his followers in the village and subject to arrest by the village police. These last are seen converging on the village from the hills, reinforced by other police, perhaps a preview of the events in Czechoslovakia later that year. Schorm has not been active since the invasion.

Jan Nemec, the director of Martyrs of Love, has been a close colleague of Schorm and shares some of his pessimistic concern over the role of the individual. This is reflected in Nemec's surrealistic film, The Party and the Guests. The plot is peculiar: a group of well-dressed, conforming people are threatened, then taken to an outdoor banquet by a sinister host. When one of the guests--acted by Evald Schorm-- leaves, the host sends out dogs and guards to retrieve him. Through the film's symbolism, Nemec implies that the banquet is the security which society offers to those who accept its power to make decisions for them, the host is government, and the escaping guest represents the individual who abandons security in order to make his own decisions.

Jan Kadar, in his well-known drama, <u>The Shop on the
High Street</u>, also used a defiant anti-hero to express his feelings about the role of the individual in society. The film,
released in 1965, centers on the unwillingness of a Czech
Fascist functionary in a small town to follow ideological necessity and rid the town of an old, deaf Jewish shopkeeper.
Kadar's study is deeply introspective, unlike the films of
Schorm and Nemec, since it is clear that the central character is torn internally between his desire to follow the dictates
of fascism and his basic Czech humanism. Kadar ends the
film on a tragic note: having decided to save the old woman,
the fascist accidentally kills her. This melodramatic finale
blunts the political message of the film, perhaps purposely.
It cannot be said that the director is using occupied war-time
Czechoslovakia as a disguise for the modern Communist state
in the same way as Menzel used the setting in <u>Closely Watched
Trains</u>. The motivation of Kadar's anti-hero, however, could
be held as valid for a committed Czech Marxist, faced with
the same philosophical dilemma.

"Everything for Sale"

Andrzej Wajda, the most prolific Polish director,
turned his attention toward the artist in 1968 with the film
<u>Everything for Sale</u>. This work is reportedly a fictionalized
tribute to the last years of Zbigniev Cybulski, the popular
actor who died the previous year attempting to board a moving train while drunk. In <u>Everything for Sale</u>, Wajda points
out the artist's interest in the unattractive facets of human
existence by continually showing scenes of violence and tragedy which are discovered to be merely scenes in a film within the film; the last work of the doomed hero. The death
of the Cybulski-like character is shown to be carefully staged
and repeated several times in order to achieve the right effect. For example, an actor is accidentally injured and the
director within the film incorporates the bleeding forehead
into a fatal automobile accident. An actress, the mistress
of Wajda's hero, is shown cutting her wrists ... then the
camera pulls back to discover her on the movie set. Her
"suicide," although appropriate for the character, is also
only a scene staged for the director.

There are several possible interpretations for the complex attitude toward the artist depicted in <u>Everything for Sale</u>.

Some critics maintain that Wajda is criticizing the artist for being a sensationalist, intent on emphasizing the tragic and the unheroic. This interpretation would be in line with the Polish government's concern over the abandonment by Polish artists of the optimism of socialist realism.

The Western interpretation of Everything for Sale is that it represents an attack on the optimism of traditional socialist culture and philosophy. According to this view, Wajda is declaring that life has a side to it that is not positive, even in a socialist state. Cybulski the actor was not an ideal socialist man and his death was both sordid and tragic. In creating a balanced view of the actor's life, the film-making artist has a responsibility to incorporate this part of Cybulski into the biography, even if it seems to emphasize the unheroic, very personal aspects of life. In short, Everything for Sale is an affirmation that the artist in his work must be true to his vision of reality rather than to the dictates of state culture.

Despite the difficulties encountered by Nemec, Schorm and Trnka, many more works on the theme of the role of the individual in the socialist system were made in Eastern Europe before the invasion of Czechoslovakia in 1968. Now, with restrictions increased, these works are banned and their export forbidden, despite the lure of hard currency from Western distribution. As a result of this policy, such important works as Wajda's Everything for Sale and Schorm's Courage for Every Day have not been shown publicly in the United States. The alienation of the artist is too controversial a subject and the Czechs were too outspoken on their views before the restoration of ideological controls. The directors of Poland and Hungary may have taken the Czech experience to heart; although Wajda and others may discuss the problem in their future films, they will certainly be very cautious in doing so, allowing conflicting interpretation of their statements. It is also possible that allegory and symbolism will be used more extensively as a means to evade criticism from the Party.

Conclusions: The Pessimistic Present

Discussion of the strict censorship of certain films and the "retirements" of Schorm and Trnka leads into general conclusions on social criticism in all Eastern European films. Despite the comparatively liberal ideological climate

in Poland, Hungary and pre-invasion Czechoslovakia, it is
clear that official controls remained a serious barrier to
free expression in Eastern Europe throughout the 1960's, as
well as in the Soviet Union. The future of social criticism
in Eastern European film clearly depends far more on the
shifting attitudes of local regimes than on local artists.

        Surprisingly, there are good reasons for the regimes
to maintain a comparatively high degree of social criticism
in their national cinemas. First and foremost, these films
serve as an outlet for feelings which would otherwise be dan-
gerously suppressed. For the artist, writing or directing a
film of mildly critical content is an alternative to producing
"desk drawer" literature. If the artist is kept busy creatively
walking the thin line that divides "acceptable" criticism and
censorable criticism, he is not devoting his energies to writing more radical statements to be passed by hand throughout
the intellectual community of his country. In addition, a
writer or director gainfully employed in the motion picture
industry is not going to feel as alienated from the socialist
society as he might if such employment were barred to him.
In brief, a limited amount of allowable criticism is an encouragement to artists to play by the socialist establishment's
rules.

        For the audience as well, social criticism in films
can provide a means for the release of pent-up resentment,
particularly in the case of satires and comedies. In The
Role of My Family in the World Revolution (1971), a film by
the Yugoslav director Bata Cengic, the audience is encouraged
to smile at the antics of a family desperately trying to conform to the early days of the Communist regime by out-revo-
lutionizing the revolutionaries. Another example of this trend
was Closely Watched Trains, in which the pompous Nazi official with his unimaginative propaganda and constant assur-
ances that everything is looking better is a genuinely funny
character. If the audience can laugh at this tiresome repetitive ideologue, they will not be as likely to feel anger against
their modern "Zedniceks." Laughter and cynicism may not
be the most desirable reactions to the problems of socialist
society, but they are better than complaints and pent-up hostility. As the slogan of Kadar's Hungarian regime states it,
"Those who are not against us are with us," even if they are
cynically amused by the failures of the regime.

        Finally, there is the lure of hard currency. During
the good years of Czech film-making, 1962-1968, Czechoslovakia

produced far more films than were needed for domestic consumption. The cause of this over-production, and of Rumania's comparatively huge film-making budget, is the export
market. During the 1960's, films were the best-known ex-
ports to the West from both Czechoslovakia and Rumania, although Rumania's export is limited to Western Europe rather
than the West in general. With these traditions and the profitable examples of War and Peace, Knife on the Water and
Closely Watched Trains as a guide, it is likely that some of
the regimes of Eastern Europe may be willing to sacrifice a
portion of their ideological control in order to reach those
profitable Western markets. They can appreciate that such
films as Anna, the Proletarian (Czech, 1952) and other mas-
terpieces of socialist realism are not likely to attract the
same large European audiences as applauded Lotna.

On the other hand, a strong case can be made against
the continuance of social criticism in the films of the area.
To the ideological conservatives of the socialist regimes, the
productive years of Eastern European film-making were years
of self-indulgent excesses on the part of directors and writers.
Party officials complain about "the cult of the director" super-
seding cooperation on the movie set and replacing the Party's
role in social commentary. In almost all of the seven countries under discussion, the trend of the last three years seems
to have been towards a reluctant mildly Stalinist position in
cultural affairs.

The Czech situation is obvious. Milos Forman was
not the only Czech director to decide, with justice, that the
years following the 1968 invasion would be difficult for the
creative Czech artist. Unlike Forman, most of the other
members of the film-making community have remained in
Prague, but the Film School has been closed and many film
workers cannot find work. Recent Czech production shows a
greater emphasis on frivolity and an absence of that serious
discussion of the problems of the individual which characterized Czech cinema of the 1960's.

In Bulgaria, Rumania and Albania, there has been little change in the content, style or political impact of films
since the death of Stalin and there is little likelihood that the
1970's will be different. All three countries are under the
firm control of Stalinist leaders; all three maintain relatively
stable cultural policy. There are very few intellectuals to
revolt against socialist realism and this insures that intellectual ferment will be met with immediate reprisals. It can

therefore be expected that Rumania and Albania will continue
to produce historical spectacles and socialist realist films,
while Bulgaria will continue to take advantage of the similarities between Bulgarian and Russian languages and depend primarily on the Soviet studios to supply motion pictures for the
Bulgarian market.

In Hungary, since the Czech invasion of 1968, the
forces of creativity and social criticism have suffered from
the neo-Stalinist reaction. Zoltan Fabri's most recent films
have been described abroad as "too literary," signifying a
return to the Hungarian tradition of filming "acceptable" classic literature. Miklos Jancso and Istvan Gaal have not worked
in their homeland for almost three years, although they have
both been active in Italy. Reports that ideological controls of
culture are tightening in the Party seem to agree with the
present conditions in Hungarian film-making.

A similar trend has appeared in Yugoslavia since 1971
when distribution of Dusan Makavejev's WR--Mysteries of the
Organism (1971) was banned. The director of Murder of a
Switchboard Operator had outraged the Yugoslav censors with
his virtually pornographic portrayal of a sexual liberationist
in his latest work. Mysteries of the Organism was also flagrantly anti-Communist. Its weak story line of sexual adventure is interrupted frequently by montage images associating
Marx and Lenin with torture. Makavejev even had his outlandish heroine declare: "You serve a lie--the Party and the
People." The Makavejev Affaire has mushroomed in the past
two years to embrace criticism of all Yugoslav directors and
artists who have lost touch with the political and ethical values
of the Titoist regime.

Poland remains a special case. On the eve of the
1970's, the situation did not look bright. Party First Secretary Gomulka, always annoyed by the liberalism of the Lodz
film-makers, was still attacking the directors as a group.
In 1971, Aleksander Ford lost his position as artistic head
of the film industry as a result of the anti-Semitic campaign
of General Mieczyslaw Moczar's faction of the Party. Ford
responded by emigrating to Israel, pausing en route to direct
a British production of the anti-Stalinist novel, The First
Circle (1972).

The ouster of Gomulka and the triumph of the Gierek
faction of the Party over Moczar in December, 1971, has
been a mixed blessing for Polish cinema. On the one hand,

the comparative liberalism of the Gierek regime has resulted
in an acknowledgment of the director's role as the prime de-
cision-maker in determining the content of his work.   This
was evidenced by the recent controversy over Wajda's latest
motion picture, The Wedding (1972).   Wajda had begun filming a screen version of a novel by the 19th-century author
Wyspianski but had decided to depart from the original classic in order to produce a work more consistent with his own
views.   The release of the film divided the Party's cultural
units into those who condemned the director for "mutilating"
a Polish classic and those who felt that Wajda was correct.
The debate ended early in 1973 with Wajda's creativity being
applauded by the Polish press--a victory for the creative independence of all Polish film-makers.

On the other hand, the Gierek regime has evidenced a
strong perference for traditional socialist realism.   This was
shown clearly in the undue amount of praise given to Jan
Rybkowski's production of another Polish classic, The Peasants (1972).   The production was noticeably inartistic, but
remained faithful to socialist realist principles regarding the
presentation of peasant life in a socialist state.   The Polish
press claimed that Rybkowski's film proved that "an insufficient artistry of form may be compensated by social values."
Copernicus (1972), a biography of the Renaissance Polish scientist filmed by Ewa and Czeslaw Petelski, also reflects socialist realist style and content.   There is no attempt to humanize the character of the great astronomer-mathematician.
Instead, the Petelskis celebrate his patriotism, making him
more of a political figure than an intellectual.   The ambiva-
lent policy demonstrated by these contrasting trends may result in future conflict.   Nevertheless, Polish cinema will
probably not overstep the limits of socialist propriety as the
Czech film-makers did during the mid-1960's and as Dusan
Makavejev did in 1971.   For this reason, Poland may continue to be a limited sanctuary for social commentary in
Eastern European film.

CHAPTER 8

CINEMA OF THE FANTASTIC AND UTOPIAN

The historical Count Drakula was an unusually savage
Rumanian warlord. The legend of his vampirism and the
tradition of the vampire in general comes to us from the
folklore of Eastern Europe. The werewolf and the grave
robber, two other standard characters of the horror film,
also carry Eastern European cultural passports. Even the
German Frankenstein monster has its slavic counterpart in
the Czech legend of Rabbi Low and the Golem.

The reason so many of "our" nightmare creatures
originated beyond the Danube is rooted in the bloody history
and extreme poverty of the region. As recently as the early
20th century, the only knowledge of the outside world which
the more isolated peasants ever acquired was through foreign
armies rampaging through the farmlands. In addition to frequent invasions, the region was blighted by epidemics, blood
feuds, starvation and ignorance. The Orthodox religion which
dominated Eastern Europe is mystical and other-worldly by
itself; in practice, it existed side-by-side with pagan beliefs
in witchcraft, gypsy curses and black magic. Almost every
village had its resident witch for fortune-telling and herb
medicines; every isolated family or clan maintained its own
tradition of an ancestor being confronted with the supernatural.
Given this social and cultural background, it is not surprising
that the mind of the more primitive peasant was filled with
the dark images that people Western horror films.

In Eastern Europe, there has been remarkably little
interest in portraying the supernatural in motion pictures.
The urban, Westernized film-makers of the region have not
enjoyed being reminded that a portion of their nations' population believed in "such things." During the period of inten-
sive nationalism between the wars, the portrayal of national
folklore in Eastern Europe was considered a blow to the national prestige because it emphasized the most backward

aspects of national culture. In the Soviet Union, of course, motion pictures using supernatural legends as subject matter were out of the question. When the film industry was mobilized in support of the socialist future, it became reactionary to encourage interest in the past by using folkloric themes.

There were exceptions to this rule in the cinema of Hungary, Poland and Czechoslovakia. No nationalist stigma was attached to films in those countries which depicted the folklore of other nations or "classic" works involving the supernatural. For example, the first film version of Bram Stoker's novel, Dracula, was produced in Hungary in 1921, one year before the more famous German Nosferatu and nine years before Hungarian-born Bela Lugosi created the role on a Universal Pictures sound stage. Pushkin's ghostly Gothic tale, "Queen of Spades," was a very popular theme for early motion pictures in Europe. Two Russian productions and one Hungarian are counted among the eight screen versions of the story produced between 1910 and 1927. The second Russian version, released in 1916, was one of the early films of the director Yakov Protazanov, destined to become a leader of the early Soviet cinema in the 1920's.

The Eastern European audience became more receptive to the purely escapist film during the 1930's, perhaps as a means to forget the Depression and the approaching threat of war. Most of the "horror" films shown in Eastern Europe during this decade were Hollywood productions, but a small number of unusually well-directed works on supernatural themes were made locally as well. A group of Czech and French film-makers collaborated on an elaborate production based on the legend of the Golem, an artificial man reputedly created by a Medieval rabbi of Prague. The film, completed in 1935, borrowed heavily from an earlier version of the same story produced in Berlin by UFA. The Golem was followed in 1937 by two Polish films, Dr. Faustus and The Dybbuk. Both of these works were designed to create a richly supernatural atmosphere within a distinctively Polish setting. The Dybbuk, a story of the possession of a young Jewish girl by an evil spirit, is particularly interesting at the present time because of its similarities with recent U.S. films such as The Other (1972) and The Exorcist (1973).

Aleksandr Ptushko and Soviet Fantasy

        In Stalin's Russia, imaginative art was limited primar-
ily to works for children.   Children's literature became an
outlet for the creative energies of writers who were either
unable to join the Communist Party or were afraid to become
involved in intra-Party struggles.   The same was true, to a
limited extent, for talented non-party directors working in
children's film-making.   Chief among these non-Party directors during the 1930's was a former puppeteer of peasant
origin: Aleksandr Lukich Ptushko.

        Ptushko, like the Czech Jiri Trnka, was quick to see
the possibilities for combining film with puppetry.   Unlike
Trnka, however, Ptushko was fascinated by the technical aspects of motion pictures.   During the early 1930's, he devised his own method of using live actors and animated pup-
pets together in the same scene, much as Merian C. Cooper
did in King Kong (1933).   In 1935, Ptushko used his special
effects technique for the production of The New Gulliver, the
first full-length Russian fantasy film to have the benefit of
sound.   For this work, which featured revolutionary Gulliver
liberating the Lilliputian proletariat from their oppressive
rulers, he received the title of Honored Artist from the Soviet government, a rare award for a non-Party member.
Outside the Soviet Union, The New Gulliver was praised by
those critics who could stomach the garish ideology for the
charm of Ptushko's animated puppet Lilliputians.

        Throughout the next ten years, Ptuskho remained the
single most important children's film-maker in the Soviet
Union.   During the war years, he was unable to work on
feature films; the needs of the state at war did not include
the entertainment of the young.   In 1946, with the help of
captured German equipment, he undertook two major films.
The first, The Stone Flower, was completed in 1946.   The
second, The Magic Voyage of Sinbad, was to be Ptushko's
last feature until 1951.   As in The New Gulliver, the original Arabian Nights' story of Sinbad's adventures was distorted
out of recognition by the ideological content.   In Ptushko's
version, Sinbad observes the great despair which has fallen
on his city because of its poverty, and he sails to find the
legendary Phoenix.   He and his crew hope that the famous
singing of the creature will bring his people out of their depression.   Arriving in India, Sinbad learns that the Phoenix
is owned by a greedy Sultan; he accepts Sinbad's gifts but

refuses to show the creature to the visitors.   Changing his
tactics, Sinbad and his crew fight their way into the chamber
of the Phoenix in the hope of stealing the prize from the evil
Sultan.

The Phoenix itself is one of Ptushko's most imaginative
creations.   In his conception, the Phoenix is a large bird
with the head and voice of a beautiful, sad-faced woman.   Its
song promises peace and rest from toil--through death--and
exerts a hypnotic effect on Sinbad's crew.   Sinbad, however,
is immune to the spell.   He rouses his men by angrily denouncing the Phoenix for singing of hopelessness and despair.
Using the Phoenix as a weapon, he and his crew rout the
evil Sultan's army and escape to sea.   When they return
home, they pledge themselves to escape from depression
through hard work and building for the future.

The parallels between Sinbad's city and post-war Russia are obvious even to a child--which was precisely the purpose of the film.   Faced with widespread destruction and despair, the Party wished to institute a mood conducive to rebuilding the nation.   Since children were to be enlisted in the
reconstruction effort, they had to be targets of at least some
of the propaganda campaign.   In their fantasy films during
this period, the political content remained dominant.

During the culturally barren years of the late 1940's,
Aleksandr Ptushko became an instructor of animation techniques at Moscow and Leningrad.   He retired from active
film-making in the mid-1950's, but his success as a teacher
can be seen in the work of Aleksandr Row, who has replaced
the late Ptushko as the single most important children's film-
maker.   Row and other Soviet directors, either alone or in
co-production with Finland and Eastern Europe, began to work
with themes from folk tales of the supernatural as early as
1959 in the production of The Day the Earth Froze.   An interesting recent development has been the production of several films centering on the supernatural and aimed at an adult
audience.   These include the first Soviet version of Pushkin's
Queen of Spades (1960).   This recent trend reflects a growing
recognition that imaginative escapist films can play a useful
role in socialist culture.

In the other states of Eastern Europe, little work has
been undertaken in fantasy and horror films since the Second
World War, primarily for the same reasons of national pride
which kept production of such works limited during the

interwar period. The major exception has been Yugoslavia
where motion picture plots occasionally hinge upon a gypsy
curse or a vampire's nocturnal expeditions. In Czechoslovakia, a small interest in the supernatural can be noted in
the gruesome thriller, Lost Face (1964), and in aging director Otakar Vavra's recent story of witch-hunting and persecution, A Hammer for the Witches (1969). In general, however, Eastern Europe reflects the stated cultural principle of
the Polish United Worker's Party: "old schemes of peasant
culture did not allow fulfillment of national aspirations and
have been abolished." A determination to forget the peasant
past still dominates film-makers and causes them to choose
subjects far removed from the supernatural.

Socialism and Science Fiction: Aelita

        If folk tales of the supernatural reflect the imagination
of the Eastern European peasant, then science fiction and utopian fiction represent the imagination of the urban intelligentsia.
Science fiction has remained a popular literary form since
the beginning of the century. Among the most noted writers
of the genre have been the Czech novelist Karel Capek and
the Soviet authors Aleksei N. Tolstoy and Aleksandr P.
Kazantsev.

        As in the West, science fiction film did not become a
major art form in most of Eastern Europe until after the
Second World War. Although the intellectuals of the region
constituted an appreciative audience for science fiction novels,
especially the classics of the French author Jules Verne, the
intelligentsia as a class was not large enough to make utopian
films profitable. Outside the intelligentsia, there was very
little interest for stories set in the distant future. For the
most part, the societies of interwar Eastern Europe were in
the stage of development known as "agrarian-traditional." In
traditional societies, the population is not very concerned with
any future event more distant than the next harvest. Such a
society is described by sociologists as lacking a "future orientation." For this reason, a film describing space flight or
any aspect of life in the remote future would not have been
appreciated by the Eastern European movie audiences.

        The logical exception to this rule during the interwar
period was the Soviet Union. After a successful revolution,
the task of any communist party is to build towards a socialist state of the future. By definition, any society under

the management of a communist party becomes a "future-
oriented" society. In the Soviet Union, this emphasis on the
future can be seen in the institution of the Five-Year Plan
and in propaganda which promises a bright socialist future
of peace and plenty in return for the sacrifices and discipline
of the present. As a result, interest in producing films that
display a utopian future can be traced back in Soviet motion
picture history to 1924, when Yakov Protazanov directed
Aelita.

    Aelita is an unusual film and Yakov Protazanov was
an unusual Soviet director. He was born in Moscow in 1881
and his early life was spent within the French-speaking intellectual community of pre-war Russia. By 1909, however,
he was known as one of the handful of directors who were
demanding the establishment of a Russian national cinema in
opposition to the imitation French films produced in Russia
by French producers which were then in vogue. During the
war years, Protazanov carried out his nationalist ideas
through a series of literary adaptations. These included an
early version of Tolstoy's War and Peace (1915) and the
Gothic mystery, Queen of Spades (1916), mentioned earlier.
Protazanov fled Russia shortly after the October Revolution
and began a brief, unfruitful career as a film-maker in
Paris. In 1923, he decided to return to Moscow where film-
making on a large scale was being resumed. Apparently,
Protazanov expected that the new Soviet industry would have
need of experienced directors such as himself.

    His first months home in Moscow must have been very
difficult. Although Protazanov was only 42, he found himself
competing with a new generation of much younger, politically-
committed film-makers. His production of the new novel
Aelita by the young radical author Aleksei Tolstoy may have
been designed to win him acceptance from his younger colleagues. In directing the film, Protazanov used the most
recent theories of "constructivist" set design, a decision
which earned him the praise of the students at the Moscow
State Film Institute and the attention of art critics throughout
the West. The costuming of Aelita was equally radical, but
is universally acknowledged as far more tasteful and believable than the Hallowe'en uniforms worn by Flash Gordon and
company fifteen years later. Considering the budget limita-
tions forced on the director by the shaky state of the Soviet
economy, Aelita was a brilliant work of artistic experimentation.

Fig. 22. Robot revolution from Protazanov's <u>Aelita</u>. Courtesy, Museum of Modern Art.

Protazanov was not nearly as creative with the story
of Aelita, although he did depart to a great extent from Tolstoy's mystical narrative of Atlantis transplanted on Mars.
In Protazanov's version, a Soviet engineer named Los designs
a spaceship and travels to Mars in company with Gushev, a
Red Army soldier and a detective.   On the Red Planet, they
discover a population transformed into robots by a tyrannical
scientific aristocracy.   The daughter of the Martian ruler,
Princess Aelita--the name approximates the word "elite" in
Russian--falls in love with Los, who educates her in humanism.   In the meantime, Gushev has roused the enslaved
Martian proletariat to revolt against the upper classes.   As
the revolution reaches its dramatic climax, Los suddenly
awakens--the whole adventure was merely a dream caused by
overwork on behalf of the Soviet state.

The propaganda message lacks subtlety, but the attention of the audience is maintained by the exotic setting and
the imaginative plot of the melodrama.   The success of
Aelita's social comment is dependent on little touches of detail and characterization, similar to the technique which
Pudovkin would use in Storm over Asia four years later.   In
Aelita, Tuscoob, the ruler, and other aristocrats are made
to appear cold and haughty and clearly unsympathetic.   The
Martian workers, on the other hand, appeal to the audience's
sympathy because of their identical uniforms and the cumber-
some steel masks they are forced to wear, hiding their human features.   Among the Martians, only Princess Aelita
has a distinctive personality.   In the most imaginative scene
of the film, for example, Aelita looks at Earth through a
massive telescope and is delighted to find a couple kissing.
She eagerly decides to experiment with the newly-discovered
custom on an impassive fellow aristocrat and is visibly disappointed with the result.   Later, she discovers that her
alien lover, Los, is not nearly as cold when she repeats the
experiment with him.   This helps considerably Los' teaching
in humanism.

Aelita was classified as an entertainment film rather
than a political film, despite Protazanov's attempt to act as
a propagandist.   During the late 1920's, Aelita was repressed
for emphasizing the fantastic too strongly and for using "un-
realistic" sets and costumes--the very aspects of the film
that made it attractive to both Russian and foreign audiences.
Today, prints of Aelita are extremely rare and it is almost

never shown publicly, due to the fragility of the film material used in 1924.

Protazanov briefly received the admiration of his colleagues, but he failed to win the trust and respect of the Party. In communist terms, his bourgeois attitudes were clearly stronger than his revolutionary zeal. After Aelita, he specialized in directing drawing-room comedies, devoid of experimentation and social comment. He was never permitted to become a member of the Communist Party, but his skill as a director earned him enough credit as a filmmaker for him to remain active until his death in 1943.

Later Soviet Science Fiction

Following the suppression of Aelita during the late 1920's, Soviet film-makers became reluctant to discuss the possibilities of converting any of the large number of Soviet science fiction novels into film. Socialist realism under Zhdanov declared that the future was "unreal" and therefore unacceptable as a setting for Soviet films. It was also said that interest in the end product of socialism was counterproductive to the needs of the Soviet state because it distracted workers from the task of building the new order. For these reasons, virtually no science fiction films were produced in the Soviet Union until the late 1950's.

In 1959, a relatively unknown director named Aleksandr Kosir completed the first of the new Soviet "utopian" films, a primitive, low-budget work entitled The Heavens Call. Released only two years before the flight of the first Russian cosmonaut, Kosir's narrative of space exploration in 2001 enjoyed unusual popularity within the Soviet Union. It has been followed by several other futuristic works, based primarily on recent science fiction novels. These include Planet of Storms (1962), Madmen's Trial (1962), The Andromeda Cloud (1968) and Amphibian Man (1962), the last evidently being a Soviet counterpart of The Creature from the Black Lagoon. In each case, the most recent Soviet science fiction film has been more elaborate and more costly than its predecessors in the same genre.

Several factors contributed to the sudden re-interest in science fiction among Soviet film-makers. The liberalization of socialist realism to permit themes, plots and settings which were formerly "unacceptable" was responsible in the

sense that it provided an opportunity which had not existed
since the 1920's.   The Soviet government was also partly
responsible because of its encouragement of interest in space
flight as a result of the successful "sputnik" flights and the
"space race" with the West.   A third influence was a resur-
gence of interest in "utopianism" in popular Soviet literature,
invariably a trend-setting art form in the Soviet Union.

       The single most influential factor was probably the
impact of foreign film-makers at the height of the 1950's
"fad" for science fiction.   In addition to films from the West,
which were rarely seen in Russia, there may have also been
considerable interest in the work of a Czech colleague of
Jiri Trnka's, Karel Zeman.   In 1956, after ten years as a
puppet film director and animator, Zeman directed a live-
actor version of Jules Verne's novel, For the Flag.   In Zeman's production, the science fiction aspects of Verne--his
fascination with outlandish inventions and fabulous weapons--
were emphasized.   The Invention of Destruction (or Fabulous
World of Jules Verne) has been followed by other Verne adaptations directed by Zeman, but the first was undoubtably the
most influential in encouraging Eastern European interest in
science fiction films.   Two years later, Polish and East German film-makers collaborated on First Spaceship on Venus,
a film whose style clearly reflects Zeman's technique.   Kosir's The Heavens Call also appears to have "the Zeman
look."

       Planet of Storms was, perhaps, the first science fic-
tion film to display distinctively Soviet characteristics.   Its
director, Pavel Vladimirovich Klushantsev, was a noted author of popular science books and an experienced director of
documentaries on astronomy.   The author of the original
novel of the same name contributed the screenplay of the
film.   A former engineer, Aleksandr P. Kazantsev had turned
to science fiction writing in the late 1940's.   Together, the
director and the author attempted to make the story of the first
Russian expedition to Venus as true to their scientific expec-
tations as possible.   Despite the resulting semi-documentary
style, Planet of Storms has some very exciting moments.
The cosmonauts are menaced by large bounding lizards and
are rescued from a lava flow by their remote-controlled robot.   At every crisis, the explorers are able to triumph
through the use of superior technology and their cooperative
efforts.   Unfortunately, the emphasis on realistic technology
was lost in the American release, Voyage to a Planet of
Prehistoric Women (1966), which added a race of scantily-
clad sirens to the Venusian landscape.

Fig. 23. Cosmonauts leaving Venus in <u>Planet of Storms.</u> (Source: Iskusstvo)

In the more advanced nations of Eastern Europe, the
style of science fiction films generally parallels that suggested
by Planet of Storms. Significantly, in socialist science fiction plots, there is never a personality conflict between the
space explorers. In Ikarie XB-1, a 1963 Czech galactic voyage, the only human problem occurs when a cosmonaut goes
temporarily mad from radiation fever. Another major difference between socialist science fiction and the Western variety
is the absence of the traditional menace of enemy aliens.
According to the Marxist theory of history, every advanced
society undergoes the same stages of development as its technology improves. By definition, any society capable of developing the technology of space flight is automatically socialist and peaceful. In Ikarie XB-1, this idea is carried to
its extreme possibilities: the Ikarus and her crew, whose
adventures the audience have been following, are discovered
to be from another planet and are traveling to Earth in peaceful exploration rather than vice versa. In the final scene,
the director has succeeded in combining a surprise ending
with the promise that any intelligent being will be true to
Marxist principles of cooperation and nonviolence.

Utopianism and Humor in Czechoslovakia

Not every Czech science fiction film follows the
Ikarie XB-1 pattern. The Czech director Oldrich Lipsky, in
the tradition of Karel Capek's black comedies, has often combined the fantastic with the commonplace for comic effect.
His first important science fiction comedy was Man from the
First Century (1961). Milos Kopecky, a popular Czech comic
actor, played a man of our time who accidently arrives on
Earth in the distant future. Finding himself in a socialist
utopia, he is unable to cope with the absence of money and
the changes in technology. Kopecky foolishly spends his
credit allowance on expensive frivolities including several
identical sport cars and a giraffe. Trying to impress a girl
during a romantic evening, he is unable to program the com-
puter to serve lobster until he presses the wrong button and
is deluged with a flood of lobsters. In a short time, his
greed and desire for position corrupt a handful of the people
around him and, as punishment, the time traveler is returned
to our time.

It is difficult to decide who Lipsky is satirizing in
Man from the First Century, since so much of the humor
depends on Kopecky's struggles with various machines.

Clearly, the time traveler is not a positive character, but his reactions to the utopian society can be seen as typical of any modern man. By the end of the film, the audience can easily sympathize with the plight of Kopecky, exiled out of an earthly paradise for being all too human in his sense of values.

A later film by Lipsky, I Killed Einstein, Gentlemen (1970) follows in the Capek tradition of emphasizing the black humor of world-catastrophe by depicting life after a nuclear war. The aftermath of the Third World War has become a relatively popular theme for Czech science fiction, as evidenced by Jan Schmidt's surrealistic End of August at Hotel Ozone (1965) and Juro Jakubisco's film of the struggle for survival among the refugees, The Deserters and the Nomads (1969). All three films are politically important in their pessimistic suggestion that the utopian future promised by socialism is not guaranteed. This idea runs counter to the Marxist concept of history inevitably moving towards communist perfection. In their themes, Lipsky, Schmidt and Jakubisco are therefore contradicting the socialist ethic. Clearly, their political and social philosophy is closer to that expressed by the new wave cinema of Czechoslovakia in the 1960's than that symbolized by the utopian, technology-oriented science fiction of the Soviet Union.

Conclusions

Film historian John Baxter has stated that "No single aspect of its cinema so accurately reflects a country's preoccupations as that of fantasy." This is clearly true for the Eastern European cinema. Each country and each period has produced fantasy and science fiction which reflects the social and political background of the time. Aelita, with its combination of bourgeois and radically revolutionary elements, could only have been produced under the special social conditions of the Soviet Union in the 1920's when bourgeois artists like Protazanov attempted to outdo the new generation in revolutionary ardor. Ptushko's "innocent" children's fantasies were not innocent of Stalinist influence, and the technology-oriented space voyages of Klushantsev and Jindrich Polak, the director of Ikarie XB-1, would not have been filmed in Eastern Europe if Communism had not supplied the area with a "future orientation." In essence, the history of the fantasy and science fiction film in Eastern Europe underscores the concept that all genres of the motion picture are strongly influenced by the political climate in which the picture was filmed.

CHAPTER 9

CINEMA AND IDEOLOGY

In the fall of 1902, the Pleograph Company of Warsaw opened the first motion picture studio in Eastern Europe. Although the firm went bankrupt the following year, this date is usually taken as the birth of cinema beyond the Danube. In the seventy years since that event, the region has known very little peace. States have been created and destroyed, boundaries shifted, peoples transferred from the rule of one government to another like so many pawns in a vast game of chess throughout our century. Governments have risen and fallen with frightening frequency, carrying whole social systems down with them. Hungary, for example, has been a kingdom, a republic, a Soviet republic, a "regency," a fascist state and a socialist state within the lifetime of many of its citizens.

It was inevitable that the motion picture, with its great promise as a propaganda instrument, would be captured by the political forces in such an environment. The transformation of cinema into a political tool followed a definite pattern in each of the Eastern European states, with the exception of Czechoslovakia. Basically, independent film studios in the region discovered that they could not finance modern feature production without some form of government assistance because the markets in each country were too small. Direct competition with the studios of Berlin, Paris and Hollywood was impossible. In each instance, initial government intervention was of absolute necessity to the Eastern European film-makers, although the form of intervention varied from occasional government subsidy, as in interwar Poland, to complete financial backing and import protection, as in the Soviet Union. Since all of the governments of Eastern Europe had a desperate need to propagandize, the government support eventually became conditional on the promotion of government policy objectives by the film industry. Czechoslovak film was able to escape from political control only by exploiting the export trade during the interwar period,

much as Sweden continues to do today. A portion of Prague
cinema, however, was captured by the forces of Slovak nationalism purely for idealistic reasons.

There is nothing intrinsically good or evil in the use
of film as propaganda. Such works as <u>Potemkin</u>, <u>Chapayev</u>
and <u>Ordinary Fascism</u> in the Soviet Union and <u>Z</u> and <u>Casa-
blanca</u> in the West prove that a propaganda film can be an
artistic work even when its political values are extremely
obvious. Nevertheless, creativity can be damaged when the
propaganda content of a film is allowed to get out of the director's control, completely overshadowing all other considerations. This has often happened in Eastern Europe; in
Hungary during the early 1940s and throughout the region
whenever Zhdanovist socialist realist principles have been
imposed.

Ideology: Degree of Government Control

There exist three levels of government control over a
national film industry for political purposes. Each level is
characterized by a method of organization and each has been
used at one time or another in Eastern Europe. The lowest
level of control is that of coordinating the political content of
motion pictures through a government-sponsored industry committee or organization. Such organizations, although theoret-
ically lying outside of the government bureaucracy, are supposedly receptive to official "guidance" on political content.
Examples of this type of organization include Bela Kun's Motion Picture Directorate and the various War Film Boards
which appeared in the Allied nations during the Second World
War. The history of cinema would seem to indicate that this
method of control is effective only when the film-makers are
already in agreement with the regime's policies and objectives.
Thus, the War Film Boards were highly successful in the coordination of the wartime propaganda effort because the film-
makers were clear as to the policy required and because they
were emotionally committed to the war effort. The Motion
Picture Directorate was not effective as a propaganda instrument, partly because it was too short-lived and partly because the film-makers had no clear commitment to the policies they were supposed to support in their films.

Strict censorship of completed works constitutes a
second level of control. Censorship can consist of editing
portions out of the film or can constitute a complete banning

of distribution of the entire work. In either case, the basic
principle remains the same; the government feels that it has
made a concession to liberalism by allowing film-makers to
work without governmental guidance, yet continues to protect
itself and the motion picture audience through direct intervention in the content of films shown. This, the most common
means of control of political content, characterizes, among
other times and places, the interwar Polish cinema and the
cinema in Yugoslavia since the early 1960s.

As a means of control, censorship is relatively effective, inexpensive and acceptable to the general public, but it
has several drawbacks. It tends to become arbitrary once
the organs of censorship have developed into a bureaucracy.
The bureaucratic censor, ill-equipped to administer consistent standards in judging the acceptability of political material, may overreact, as in the case of interwar Poland, or be
too lax from the regime's viewpoint, as was clearly the case
in Czechoslovakia during the mid-1960s. Either tendency attacks the creative process by making the limits of political
propriety too vague to follow. The result is often an exodus
of the more creative workers from the industry, either
abroad or to other art forms. At the same time, second-
rate directors who have a knack for avoiding the censor tend
to dominate the national cinema.

The third, most thorough method of control is to install government ideologists as supervisors at every level of
production. This is occasionally in force only in one government-owned studio in the event that the government studio
competes with privately-owned film companies. Thus, in
the Soviet Union during the mid-1920s, only the government-
owned Sovkino studio was under direct ideological supervision;
the other studios were subject to censorship but remained independent. More commonly, however, the government will
assume complete control of the entire national film industry
and install ideologists on every studio set. This method demands a vast bureaucracy, completely reliable from the
ideological viewpoint. Only a highly organized ideological
movement such as a totalitarian political party can sustain
this form of political control over a national film industry.
For this reason, only the Soviet Union and Eastern Europe
under Stalin and his immediate successors and Germany under the final years of Nazi rule were able to marshall sufficient resources to achieve this total control of the industry.

The drawbacks to complete domination of the film

industry by ideologists with little or no training in motion
picture techniques are obvious. When all content is determined by personnel not directly involved in the creative process, film-makers are often reduced to the status of mere
technicians carrying out assignments handed down from the
Party. The resulting motion pictures are usually ineffective,
either as entertainment or propaganda. Dissatisfaction among
the intelligentsia increases as their role in the creative process decreases, forcing them out of the film industry. As
noted in earlier chapters, this was the precise situation
which led to the "scenario crisis" in Soviet cinema throughout Stalin's lifetime.

        Despite these drawbacks, the benefits of extremely
tight control continue to make it attractive to "hard-line"
ideologues. To a true revolutionary, all aspects of society
that cannot be integrated into the Cause are non-productive
or, at best, bourgeois. If this assumption is made, it follows that the only cinema which is useful is political in nature; this is the basis for the original "Lenin proportion."
The political content of Ptushko's children's fantasies and the
condemnation by the Zhdanovist extremists of the humor in
Jazz Comedy as "apolitical empty laughter" can best be explained by this line of thought. The logical conclusion of
this logic is that good Party status is far more important to
the film-maker than talent, since the true importance of the
motion picture is its adherence to Party doctrine and its
ability to reflect "correct" political principles. Judging the
quality of cinema as art is "bourgeois" and secondary. In
effect, the successful continuance of the revolution demands
the supremacy of ideologists over the artists in all phases
of national cinema.

                                               Hable espanol

Ideology: The Artist's Contribution

        The ideological content of motion pictures is not solely
dependent upon governmental control of the industry, except
where such control approaches totality. Film-makers have
political convictions of their own which are expressed in their
works, despite censorship and other barriers to free expansion. The film-maker's contribution to the ideological content of his work is extremely important to political analysts
because it reveals the unofficial ideology of the national intelligentsia. This, in turn, provides clues to the basic political climate.

In general, the personal convictions of Eastern European directors have tended to emphasize nationalism and liberalism. These terms must be analyzed in their Eastern context. Liberalism, for example, does not mean democracy. It does mean, however, principles of freer expression, recognition of the individual and the right to dissent from the majority. Nationalism as an ideology is usually directed against one of the neighboring states and is reflected in a series of centuries-long feuds: Rumania vs. Hungary, Poland vs. the Ukraine, Serbia vs. Bulgaria, etc. It may be supposed that communism has proven a unifying force; nevertheless, recent events indicate that some of these disputes continue. Other aspects of nationalism include glorification of the past national history--relatively easy since almost every state in Eastern Europe has been either a dominant power or a participant in a protracted struggle for independence--and the celebration of folk culture.

As noted in chapters three and seven, the film-makers of Czechoslovakia have been the most persistent and vocal exponents of liberal ideology in Eastern Europe. There are vast differences among the styles of Inneman, Machaty, Forman and Nemec. All four fit into a single pattern in terms of theme and ideology. Machaty in <u>Ecstasy</u> and Nemec in <u>The Party and The Guests</u> are both clearly testing the limits of expression, attempting to expand them beyond previous levels.

Czech concepts of liberal humanism are very different from Russian concepts of the same ideology, but the latter also can be traced--with difficulty--in the cinema of the Soviet Union. In recent years, the liberal traditions of the Russian intelligentsia have been observed in Soviet film versions of classic Russian literature: Tolstoy, Chekhov and Dostoyevski. Personal statements reflecting this tendency center on the depiction of the Second World War in humanistic, as opposed to political and nationalistic, terms.

The question of nationalism in Eastern European cinema since 1945 has been analyzed earlier. The point must be continually restated that nationalistic ideology is not solely the preserve of official ideologists; it is widely accepted as a value among the population of Eastern Europe as a whole. Bieganski of Poland, for example, found inspiration in the revolutionary history of his country <u>before</u> the nationalistic regime of Marshal Pilsudski came to power. Three decades later, after Nazification and Russification, Andrzej Wajda

continued in his early works the same traditional theme of
sacrificing life for the Polish homeland.

Istvan Szekely was able to combine the liberalism of
the Hungarian intellectuals with the nationalism of the Horthy
regime and the Hungarian motion picture audience. It is not
clear how much of his personal views Szekely incorporated
into his work; his later films produced in the West continued
to reflect liberal principles but failed to emphasize the romantic nationalism of Only One Night and Rakosci March. It
is interesting for political analysts to note that a similar con-
tradictory combination of nationalism and liberal humanism
can be observed in the works of Hungarian directors of the
late 1960's.

How Far Is Beyond the Danube?

Political analysis of the content of motion pictures
need not be restricted to Eastern Europe, where government
control of the film industry makes such analysis relatively
uncomplicated. Cinematic technique--including the incorpora-
tion of political content into feature films--has crossed the
cultural boundaries marked by the Danube and influenced the
cinema of the West. This tendency can be explained, in
part, by the physical transfer of personnel from the East to
the West. Hollywood is indebted to the intellectual refugees
of the 1920s and 1930s, notably Michael Curtiz, Svatopluk
Inneman, Gustav Machaty and other recruits for Paramount
and Warner Brothers studios, for maintaining creative vitality
during the transition to sound. Curtiz in particular was responsible for the European flair given to the propaganda works
of the war period: Mission to Moscow and Casablanca (both
1942) and To Have and Have Not (1943). During the past
five years, the list of directors trained in Eastern European
who have worked in the West includes Roman Polanski, Wajda,
Ford, Jancso, Milos Forman, Sergei Bondarchuk, Vlado
Kristl (a Zagreb-trained animator) and Ivan Passer (a colleague of Forman). Through these men and others, the intellectual climate of Eastern Europe manifests itself in
Western cinema.

From the viewpoint of the political analyst, the most
important aspect of the cinema of the West is not the political
contributions of Eastern European directors. Rather, the
analysis of the films of native directors of France, Italy,
Britain and the United States may prove fruitful in

understanding our own basic political culture. For example, how does the nationalism of John Wayne as a director (The Green Berets, etc.) compare with the political culture of America as a whole? Does the celebration of the vigilante in some of D. W. Griffith's work (Birth of a Nation, etc.) and in Cecil B. DeMille's This Day and Age (1933) have its basis in American ideas of justice? What political attitudes are reflected in the work of Peter Watkins--The War Game (1966), Privilege (1967), etc.?

The entire concept of examining political culture through the national cinema of a particular country is still very new. It is not certain what the limits of content analysis are; it is possible that such methods cannot be applied when cinema is divorced from governmental influence. Nevertheless, the possibilities are intriguing. It would seem that, in terms of the practice of inserting political statements into motion pictures, the West is not so very different from the politically tumultuous region beyond the Danube.

BIBLIOGRAPHY

(Works Available in English)

POLITICS IN THE CINEMA

Carter, Huntley. The New Spirit in the Cinema. New York: Arno Press, 1970. Reprint of 1930 work examining the use of film as an instrument of social criticism.

Furhammer, Leif and Folke Isaksson. Politics and Film. New York: Praeger, 1971. Translated from the Swedish. Biased but extremely valuable analysis of motion picture propaganda.

International Educational Cinematographic Institute. The Social Aspects of Cinema. Rome: The League of Nations, 1934.

Lawson, John Howard. Film in the Battle of Ideas. New York: Masses and Mainstream, 1953.

Randall, Richard. Censorship of the Movies: The Social and Political Control of a Mass Medium. University of Wisconsin Press, 1968.

EASTERN EUROPE

Hibbin, Nina. Eastern Europe: An Illustrated Guide. London: Tantivy Press; New York: A. S. Barnes, 1969. Filmography of leading directors and actors of the 1960's. A good reference work.

Manvell, Roger. New Cinema in Europe. New York: E. P. Dutton; London: Studio Vista, 1965. Good, although overly optimistic, chapter on the Soviet cinema of the Khrushchev period.

Whyte, Alistair. New Cinema in Eastern Europe. New York:

181

E. P. Dutton; London: Studio Vista, 1971. Omits
the Soviet Union from analysis, extremely apolitical in
content.

BULGARIA

Komitet za Kinematografia. Bulgarian Cinematography.
Sofia: Bulgarian National Committee for Cinematography, 1953.

Racheva, Maria. Present-Day Bulgarian Film. Sofia:
Committee for Cinematography, 1964. Excellent national history of cinema.

CZECHOSLOVAKIA

Bocek, Jaroslav. Jiri Trnka: Artist and Puppet Master.
Prague: Artia, 1965.

Zalman, Jan. Films and Film-Makers in Czechoslovakia.
Prague: Orbis, 1968. Out of print.

Zvonicek, Stanislav, ed. Modern Czechoslovak Film 1945-
1965. Prague: Artia, 1965. Translated from the
Czech, out of print.

HUNGARY

Nemeskurty, Istvan. Word and Image: History of the Hungarian Cinema. Budapest: Corvina, 1968. Translated
from the Hungarian, an excellent national history.

Tabori, Paul. Alexander Korda. London: Oldbourne, 1959;
New York: Living Books, 1966. Early chapters provide insight into Hungarian cinema of the 1910's.

POLAND

Banaskiewicz, Wladyslaw. Contemporary Polish Cinematography. Warsaw: Polonia Publishing House, 1962. Not
nearly as authoritative as Banaskiewicz's untranslated
three volume history of Polish cinema. Out of print.

Butler, Ivan. The Cinema of Roman Polanski. London:
    Tantivy Press; New York: A. S. Barnes, 1970.

Grzelecki, Stanislaw. Polish Films Today. Warsaw:
    Polonia Publishing House, 1954.

    "Lettres Modernes" of Paris has recently published
several studies of individual Polish directors. These have
not been translated into English as of 1973.

SOVIET UNION

Arossev, A., ed. Soviet Cinema. Moscow: VOKS, 1935.

Babitsky, Paul, and John Rimberg. The Soviet Film Indus-
    try. New York: Praeger, 1955. Babitsky's contribu-
    tions are invaluable for the study of the industry under
    Stalin.

Cherkassov, Nikolai. Notes of a Soviet Actor. Moscow:
    Foreign Language Publishing House, 1957. Pro-
    Stalinist narrative of the same period covered by
    Babitsky.

Dickinson, Thorold, and Catherine de la Roche. Soviet
    Cinema. New York: Arno Press, 1972. Reprint of
    1948 work.

Leyda, Jay. Kino: A History of the Russian and Soviet
    Film. New York: Hillary House, 1960. Concentrates
    on aesthetic developments and stylistic changes, lacks
    political analysis.

Lisorvesky, D. One Hundred Soviet Films. Moscow:
    Iskusstvo, 1967.

Moussinac, Leon. Serge Eisenstein. New York: Crown
    Publishers, 1969. Translated from the French.

Seton, Marie. Sergei M. Eisenstein: A Biography. New
    York: Grove Press, 1960.

    A vast quantity of additional references are available in
Russian from Iskusstvo, the publishing house of the Soviet
film industry. These include several volumes of collected
screenplays and several important autobiographies.

184 Cinema Beyond the Danube

The French firm of "Editions Seghers" has published
an excellent series of biographies of Soviet directors. These
are not available in translation.

YUGOSLAVIA

Brenk, France. A Brief History of Yugoslav Cinema. Belgrade, 1961. Translated from the French.

Holloway, Richard. Z Is for Zagreb. London: Tantivy
Press, 1972. Excellent history of the Zagreb "school"
of animation.

PUBLISHED SCREENPLAYS

Battleship Potemkin. (U.S.S.R., 1925) London: Lorrimer
Publishing, 1968. Also available as Potemkin!, New
York: Simon and Schuster, 1968.

Closely Watched Trains. (Czech, 1966) New York: Simon
and Schuster, 1971.

Ivan the Terrible. (U.S.S.R., 1944, 1946) New York:
Simon and Schuster, 1962. Includes unproduced
Part III.

Jan Huss. (Czech, 1957) Prague: Artia, 1957. In English.

Professor Mamlock. (U.S.S.R., 1938) Excerpts in One-
Act Play Magazine, II, No. 5 (Nov., 1938), 489-495.

Strike. (U.S.S.R., 1925) Excerpt in The Film Sense by
Sergei Eisenstein. New York: Harcourt, Brace and
Co., 1942, pp. 233-235.

WR--Mysteries of the Organism. (Yugoslav, 1971) New
York: Avon Press, 1973.

MISCELLANEOUS

Manvell, Roger. The International Encyclopedia of Film.
New York: Crown Publishers, 1972.

Tyler, Parker. Classics of the Foreign Film: A Pictorial

Treasury. New York: The Citadel Press, 1962; London: Spring Books, 1966. Describes the major works of Eisenstein, Pudovkin and others.

Willis, Donald. Horror and Science Fiction Films: A Checklist. Metuchen, N.J.: The Scarecrow Press, 1972. Includes works in the genre from Eastern Europe.

Winchester, Clarence, ed. The World Film Encyclopedia: A Universal Screen Guide. London: Amalgamated Press, 1933.

Eastern European films are available for private showings from The Museum of Modern Art Collection in New York City and from Brandon Films, Inc., Chicago and White Plains, N.Y. Although more costly, the Brandon Films collection is far more complete and up-to-date and, unlike the Museum's, generally has English-dubbed and/or subtitled versions.

INDEX OF EASTERN EUROPEAN FILMS

Following title, each entry lists country of origin, year of production, director and page reference(s).

189

OTHER FILMS

Nosferatu (Germany, 1922), F. W. Murnau 161
Other, The (U.S. , 1972), Robert Mulligan 161
Privilege (U.K. , 1967), Peter Watkins and Paul Jones 179
Steamboat Willie (U.S. , 1928), Walt Disney 49
This Day and Age (U.S. , 1933), Cecil B. DeMille 179
To Have and Have Not (U.S. , 1944), Howard Hawks 178
Twelve Chairs, The (U.S. -Yugoslavia, 1970), Mel Brooks &
     Dorda Vikolic 130
2001: A Space Odyssey (U.K. , 1968), Stanley Kubrick 2
War Game, The (U.K. , 1966), Peter Watkins 179
Z (French-Algerian, 1968), Costa-Gavras 174

GENERAL INDEX

195

197